The Highland Heart in Nova Scotia

The
Highland
Heart
in Nova Scotia

Neil MacNeil

**WITH AN AFTERWORD
ON THE LIFE OF NEIL MacNEIL**

Breton Books
Wreck Cove, Nova Scotia
1998

THIS BOOK has had several editions, including Charles Scribner's Sons, reprinted by Thomas Allen, and then by Formac Publishing. Our thanks to Caroline MacGregor of Formac, for permission to offer this 50th Anniversary edition.

OUR THANKS to Neil F. MacNeil's son Neil, of Bethesda, Maryland, who provided us with photographs and details of family history. Our thanks as well to Kathleen MacKenzie, Archivist, St. Francis Xavier University, for research assistance, and to Don MacGillivray, Big Pond, for the photo of Captain Alex MacLean (Vancouver Public Library).

Editor: Ronald Caplan
Production Assistance: Bonnie Thompson
Typesetting: Glenda Watt

COVER PAINTING by Marie Moore, "View from Highland Village, Iona," is part of the "Life and Landscapes" series. Prints are available from East Coast Fine Art Prints, 1-800-565-9464. See website: www.cb-isle.com/art. Our thanks to George Gardner for permission to reproduce this painting.

**We acknowledge the support of
the Canada Council for the Arts for our publishing program.**

**We also acknowledge support from Cultural Affairs,
Nova Scotia Department of Education and Culture.**

Canadian Cataloguing in Publication Data

MacNeil, Neil, 1891-1969.

The highland heart in Nova Scotia.

ISBN 1-895415-17-9

1. Cape Breton Island (N.S.) — Social life and customs. I. Title.

FC2343.4.M36 1997   971.6'9   C97-950145-8
F1039.C2M33 1997

Contents

PHOTOGRAPHS BETWEEN PAGES 26 AND 27

One Winter Night

WHAT IS MORE BEAUTIFUL than a clear, cold, moonlit night among the snows of the North! What more sublime!

All nature is clad in its immaculate garment of white. Not a sound of any kind breaks the eloquent silence, for the winds are resting and the birds and the beasts of the forest are asleep. The trees take on fantastic shapes and cast fantastic shadows. The air is frigid and yet warm, for the blood courses through your glowing body. A million stars escort the moon in its heavenly journey and look down upon a world of peace. The countryside is bathed in silvery light, a light that belongs neither to real day nor real night. It is so bright that one can almost read a book by it; but what book could tell the story that the scene unfolds?

A man is happy to be alive and about on such a night; yet he feels meek and small, for he knows that God is close at hand.

Only the Supreme Artist could paint such a landscape!

On just such a night a few years before the turn of the century a sleigh dragged by a plodding and weary horse to the gay music of a string of silver bells left Iona in the Island of Cape Breton for the nine-mile drive to isolated and primitive Washabuckt. A child, I rode in that sleigh with my father and my younger brother, Murdoch, who later died a hero's death in World War I. We had just arrived from Boston by train after a long and tedious trip; and we were bound for the home of my Grandfather, which was destined to be my home for the next decade.

The snow enveloped everything. It sat in great heaps upon the roofs of houses and barns and deep paths had to be cut through it to the doorways. It swamped and decorated the spruce and fir trees and bent their limbs towards the earth. It filled the hollows in the meadows and the hillsides, so that rough ground appeared level and even. It covered the picket and rail fences, with only a few posts and stakes rising above it like gray ghosts, so that the fields seemed to be the common property of all men. The roads, too, were smothered in this blanket of white.

Fortunately for us, however, the old horse knew the way home, for it had made the trip to Grandfather's home many times and was intent on returning to the comfort and repose of its own stable.

It was a strange new world to me as I peeked from the warm folds of the massive buffalo robe. I was impressed both by the excessive whiteness and by the vast spaces. I had been accustomed to the crowded streets of the city with their houses built one beside the other and this was my first visit to the country. The contrast was sudden and overwhelming. I liked the jogging of the horse and the tingle of the bells and the slips and slides of the sleigh as we moved along. Once in a while we saw a little one-story cottage beside a clump of trees or in the shelter of a hill, with a dim light or two. As often as not faces appeared in the windows, for this too was a country of squinting windows.

At the start I was all attention and curiosity. My father for the most part sat as silent as the night. My three-month-old brother slept soundly, unconscious of it all, in the arms of my aunt, who had met us at the railroad station with the horse and sleigh.

The journey to Washabuckt over hills and across forests through this infinity of snow took about two hours. But it seemed like an eternity to me. I quickly tired of it. Its novelty remained; but its sameness, repeated over and over again, like the sad refrain of a Highland dirge, dulled my curiosity. My interest in its chaste patterns slackened and I was eager to be done with it. I had already decided that I liked Boston better; and I wanted to reach Grandfather's home to see what that was like.

"Where is Washabuckt?" I kept asking every few minutes.

"We'll soon be there," my aunt would reply.

"How long is 'soon'?" I would persist.

Finally my father and my aunt tired of answering my questions. Father stopped the horse and pointed into the forest.

"When you hear a big wind in the trees," he said, "you will know you are in Washabuckt."

This diverted my attention to the trees and the forest. All ears, I listened for the sound of the "big wind." It did not come and ultimately we swung around the mountain and out of the forest and drove up to the door of Grandfather's home.

Grandfather and his dog appeared in the brighter light of the door. There were others also, my Grandmother, other aunts, some relatives, and some family friends; but I shall always remember my first meeting with my Grandfather and his dog and that only. He was a commanding figure of a man, then in his middle seventies, erect and tall and strong, with a mass of tossed white hair. His strength of character impressed me from the start. I was later to learn that he could be a stern disciplinarian.

We were rushed into the house to the fireside. There we received warm food. I was sent to bed soon afterwards, but not before Grandfather had taught me the Gaelic word for dog. It is "cù." For Gaelic was the language of Grandfather's household, as it was of the countryside.

The dog's name was "Rory."

CHAPTER TWO

MacNeils and MacLeans

THE TRADITIONS AND CUSTOMS of the Scots were soon impressed upon me. Grandfather made certain of that. He, himself, was an exemplar of the Highland gentleman and that of itself would have profoundly influenced my brother and me, but besides that he took it upon himself to nurture in his two young grandsons that rare and mysterious mixture of pride and simplicity, of pugnacity and kindness, that makes the true Scot. Over and over again he told us of the glories and virtues of the Scots. He repeated the old legends of our people. He extolled Scottish triumphs, which were many, and explained away Scottish failings, which were few. For him the Scots were the best of all peoples under God, and, of course, the MacNeils were the best of the Scots.

I shall always cherish the memory of the nights, long, dark, cold, Nova Scotia nights, when he would sit in front of the big, hot kitchen stove, his stockinged but shoeless feet upon it, and with one of us grandsons upon each knee he would pour forth his soul in Gaelic songs, songs of the stormy isles, songs of the glens and the lochs, songs of battle and of victory, songs of love, songs of the Clan MacNeil. He had a good voice and enjoyed the singing as much as we did.

Thus he gave us an exalted opinion of our people, but meanwhile he kept us simple and humble as individuals.

My brother and I made apt pupils.

OUR ANCESTORS SETTLED Washabuct in 1818. They were all MacNeils and MacLeans and came from Barra, an island in the Hebrides off the west coast of Scotland. Hardy and strong, belligerent yet benevolent, Gaelic-speaking Catholics, they feared not man nor devil, and were willing to fight or love at the slightest provocation. Courageous and independent, they sought no favors from others and asked no help from any government, anywhere. They were ample unto themselves.

Barra had been the home of the MacNeils from early in the eleventh century, when they arrived there from Ireland; but how the MacLeans happened to be there has not been adequately explained and must remain one of the minor mysteries on the fringe of history. They were tolerated in Barra probably because they had married into the MacNeil families. Despite their name, they considered themselves true Barra-men and as such doubtless had more MacNeil blood than MacLean.

The Clan MacNeil of Barra is one of the oldest and proudest in Scotland, with a history, recorded and legendary, that is incredibly fantastic. The MacNeils fought everybody and everything, their neighboring clans, the Vikings, the kings of Scotland, the English, and the North Atlantic storms; and meanwhile they extricated an uncertain livelihood from fishing and piracy on their turbulent waters and from the thin, sterile soil of their windswept island. As Grandfather often remarked with pride, with them it was a real case of survival of the fittest, for only the strong, the brave and the intelligent could survive the rigors of their climate and the hardships of their life.

According to Clan legends the MacNeils descended from Niall (or Neil) of Scythia, who like Joseph was minister to the Pharaoh of Egypt, gave his name to the River Niall, or Nile, and married the Princess Scota, the daughter of the Pharaoh who rescued Moses from the bulrushes, by whom he had a daughter Gaedhal, or Gael. Whether you credit legends or not, here you have the origins of the MacNeils, the Scots and the Gaels.

Of the antiquity of the MacNeils there can be no doubt whatever, for it is proverbial in Scotland that "The MacNeils had their ain boat at the Flood," a tribute to their old age and to their seamanship and independence, all of which were common knowledge among their fellow Scots.

These ancient legends mark the progress of the Mac-Neils from Egypt to Crete and thence to Spain and finally to Ireland and Scotland. There is no space here to detail the story these legends tell of gory battles and triumphs over man and nature, but it might be noted in passing that there is scarcely an event of importance in 5000 years of tradition and history in which the Mac-Neils, seemingly, did not play a major role. If perchance the MacNeils were ever defeated in any battle or undertaking, the legends have made no note of it. Of course these are MacNeil legends.

The MacNeils of Barra trace their ancestry in direct and unbroken line to Neil of the Nine Hostages, who became King of Ireland in 379 A.D. In fact, the name Mac-Neil indicates this, for, translated into English, it means "son" of the "chief" or "king." This Neil—better known in Gaelic as Niall Mor, or Neil the Great—was the first chief of the MacNeil Clan, the present chief being the forty-fifth in unbroken male descent from him. The O'Neils of Ireland also claim descent from Neil of the Nine Hostages, the "O" or "Ui" in their name meaning "grandson" or "of the kin of."

Neil and his descendants reigned over Ireland for centuries and each king of Ireland was duly recorded as chief of the Clan MacNeil. Finally Aodh Aonrachan, or Hugh the Solitary, became King of Ireland and the twentieth chief of the MacNeils. He had a younger son Neil, named for Neil of the Nine Hostages, who led an expedition of his kinsmen to the Hebrides and settled in Barra. He thus became the first MacNeil of Barra, and the twenty-first chief of the Clan. There is some dispute about the exact year of his settling in Barra, but it was between 1030 and 1049. The first entry in the Barra Register is 1049, so it could not be later than that.

From then on the history of the MacNeils is definite and violent. They were rarely at peace with any one, and the more numerous their enemies the better they liked it. For centuries they fought the raiding Vikings, and at least three Viking kings are buried in Barra where they died. They fought in league with the Lord of the Isles, and often alone. They made commando raids against neighboring clans on the other islands or the mainland of Scotland to get loot, liquor and women. They fought for Bruce in the liberation of Scotland, with Bonnie Dundee, and with Bonnie Prince Charlie. In season and out they preyed on ships that had the temerity to sail upon Mac-Neil waters. They entered every fight they could discover, and regardless of the merits of the cause.

On occasion other clans or the forces of the kings of Scotland would attack the MacNeils in their island fastness and sometimes besiege the Chiefs in Kisimul, their castle stronghold, which was built on a tiny, rocky island in Castlebay, a sort of island within an island. Usually, however, their remoteness served them well, saving them from assault, or minimizing the assaults that came their way. There is no record of a defeat suffered by the Mac-Neils in Barra—not in the whole range of history.

This remoteness not only preserved the MacNeils

from the ravages of their foes but it also delayed the advent of Christianity, and isolated them from all the cultural movements of the world. The Chiefs, of course, had their Clan Bard and Clan Piper, the Clan Fool and the Clan Annalist, and these not only entertained the clansmen and exalted their greatness, but also made their contribution to MacNeil culture. If the MacNeils had found it necessary to interest themselves in the sciences or the humanities, they would no doubt have been successful in these as in all other matters; but they never found any need for them. Theirs was a life of action and not of contemplation; the realities of their situation left them no other choice.

Sitting in Kisimul Castle The MacNeils of Barra recognized many inferiors and no superiors. They took greatness for granted, and indeed there were few to dispute it. They reigned as the fathers of their kinsmen, not as sovereigns, for all the members of the clan were their blood kinsmen, their namesakes, and the lowest member of the community could speak up and make his wants and desires known to the Chief, and did whenever he felt like it.

All the Clansmen considered the Clan's fights and interests their individual fights and interests, and acted accordingly. Each Clansman had his share of the land and the commons and his fair share of everything there was to share. It was a patriarchal system. No one went hungry if the Chief and the Clan had food. There never was an abundance but what was available all enjoyed and when they went hungry they were all hungry together.

While all the MacNeils were equals, with special rights granted to the Chief by general approval, the lowest of the MacNeils considered himself the superior of any other living man. He felt this so deeply that he did not allow any argument about it. He bore himself with great pride, especially in the presence of strangers. He spoke with restraint and dignity, and once having spoken his mind he permitted no contradiction, except perhaps from his Chief. He was free as the eagle is free, and independent because he would not acknowledge dependence on any one or anything.

The Chiefs encouraged this great pride, and in fact gave it leadership both by example and precept. Modest and kind in their relations with their fellow Clansmen, they assumed the airs of imperial majesty in their relations with all the other rulers of the earth. Enthroned in their little island domain, about the size of Bermuda, they strutted about in regal grandeur and insisted on all the prerogatives of the great of their time.

Every night, for instance, a herald would mount the battlements of Kisimul Castle, blow a blast of a trumpet into the wild winds of the northern seas, and proclaim in Gaelic:

"Hear, oh ye peoples! Listen, oh ye nations! The Great MacNeil of Barra has finished his dinner. The other princes of the earth may now dine."

These assumptions were not always acknowledged by others and on occasion caused some merriment. It is recorded in the Carstares state papers that the Earl of Argyll, chief of Clan Campbell and one of the leading nobles of Scotland, was amused by the formality and state with which an Ambassador from the MacNeil of Barra presented him with a letter offering military support as if MacNeil "belonged to another kingdom." These papers also relate how MacNeil acted when a Spanish ship was wrecked on the rocks of Barra. As the Chief and his Clansmen were about to help themselves to both ship and cargo some one protested that the King of Spain might not like it. That, responded the Chief with awesome dignity, was something for the Chief and King to settle between themselves.

Once in a while efforts were made to curtail the activities of The MacNeils of Barra. The most notorious of these occurred during the Chieftainship of Rory the Turbulent, the thirty-fifth Chief. Rory and his men plundered an English ship off the coast of Ireland, adding considerably to his income and stores. However, Rory's exploit was not relished by Queen Elizabeth, who had just defeated the Spanish Armada, and she protested in strong terms to her kinsman, and later her successor, James VI of Scotland. She demanded that Rory be brought to justice.

James knew that this was more easily demanded than done. Realizing the difficulty of dealing with Rory by force he decided to resort to stratagem. He selected the wily Rory MacKenzie, Tutor of Kintail, for the task. They fitted out a ship as a trader and in due course it arrived in Castlebay, off Kisimul Castle. MacKenzie asked for an audience with Rory and, getting it, told him that while on the way from Norway to Ireland he had encountered a French trader and obtained a choice collection of wines. He added that he would be greatly honored if Rory would be his guest on his ship for dinner. Rory accepted the invitation and boarded the ship. He got his fill of the wines, but while enjoying them the hatches were secured, the anchor weighed and the ship and Rory headed toward Edinburgh.

James was astounded to meet a dignified and kindly gentleman with a flowing beard instead of the ruffian he had expected. The Chief on his part decided to play the courtier and to make light of the whole affair. When the king asked why he had attacked the subjects of Queen Elizabeth and their ship, Rory replied that he felt he was acting in the best interests of the King, for had not Elizabeth beheaded his mother, Mary Queen of Scots?

This clever answer placated the King. He freed Rory to return to Barra, and he rewarded MacKenzie with the superiority of the lands of Barra, forty pounds sterling a year, a hawk on demand, and military aid when required. Rory assented to all these demands until he got back to Barra, and then promptly forgot all about them. Mac-Kenzie got nothing for his wile and his efforts, but Rory the Turbulent had learned a lesson—he never again accepted an invitation to dine and wine on a ship.

It would be a base injustice to the MacNeils to assume that they were wanting in gallantry to their ladies and in chivalry to their enemies. They had their code of honor; but it was all their own. They enjoyed a good fight and they fought hard and with all they had when they did fight, but they respected courage in others. Of course they carried off what ladies they wanted on their raids but they treated them as they did their own ladies—with the greatest consideration. The MacNeils always glorified physical strength and fortitude; but they were no worse than their times. The Islands and the Highlands of Scotland in those days were no place for an effete living.

Their relish of a good fight is well illustrated in the encounter of Black Rory the Unjust and Rob Roy Mac-Gregor. The fame of Rob Roy as a swordsman finally reached the Island of Barra. Black Rory, the Chief, fancied himself as a swordsman; in fact he considered himself the superior of any other. So he set out for the Mac-Gregor territories on the mainland.

Soon after landing he met a little man riding on a horse and looking tired. Rory asked him where Rob Roy lived.

"You have him here," responded the little man, for he was none other than the dreaded terror of the Mac-Gregors.

Rory explained the purpose of his visit and challenged Rob to a duel. Rob said he was a bit weary and suggested that Rory be his guest for the night and that they fight next morning. The impatient Rory would have none of this, so Rob dismounted and the fight started, the famous duel between Red Rob and Black Rory.

Despite his arrogance Rory was no match for Rob Roy. The MacGregor had a great advantage over him in reach. Grandfather explained that Rob's arms were so long that he could tie his garters below his knee without stooping. First Rob nicked the top off Rory's ear; but Rory refused to yield. Then Rob slashed Rory's fighting arm below the elbow. Rory was then forced to quit, which he did. He generously complimented Rob Roy on his prowess. Rob in turn paid his respects to Rory, took him to his home where The MacNeil remained as an honored guest until his wounds healed.

Black Rory the Unjust and Rob Roy, the outlaw, thereupon became fast friends.

The MacNeils gloried in their exploits, which improved in the telling as they passed from one generation to another. They had a great love for Barra and for its colorful story. Few left Barra without some regrets, and rare is the one, generations later, who does not recall the misty isle with a sad heart.

How MY ANCESTORS came to leave Barra for America is variously explained, each family having its own version which differs in some respects, often important ones, from other versions. One thing is certain; they were led to Washabuckt in Nova Scotia by my great-great-grandfather, Lachlan MacLean, then ninety years old, a patriarch with qualities of greatness that equalled his years and his courage. The story as told to me by my Grandfather, which is doubtless as accurate and inaccurate as any other, follows:

Many MacNeils fought for Bonnie Prince Charlie, when he led the desperate but gallant attempt to restore the throne of Great Britain to the Stuarts. These Mac-Neils shared his victories and marched into Edinburgh with him. They were led into the Scottish capital by sixty pipers. "That was great music," remarked my Grandfather. It was their hour of triumph. Later Prince Charlie went down to ignoble and disastrous defeat at Culloden in 1746.

After this crushing defeat the Scots made their way back to their Highland and Island homes as best they could, pursued by the English hordes of the Duke of Cumberland, son of George II, and since known in Scotland as the "Butcher." Many of the straggling, half-naked, half-starved and broken-hearted Scots, the Mac-Neils among them, were slaughtered by the English or perished from their hardships. The Chief of the Mac-Neils was captured and taken to London, where he was held as a prisoner of war in the Tower.

Severe measures were imposed in an attempt to destroy the Scottish spirit and Scottish customs. The Scots were denied the right to wear the kilt. Their pipe music was proscribed. The clan system was declared illegal and efforts made to stamp it out.

The "Butcher" did his work so well that Parliament voted him an annuity of forty thousand pounds sterling in addition to his other revenues as a prince of the House of Hanover.

Lachlan MacLean was about eighteen years old at the time of Culloden. Thus he lived through the military, political and religious persecutions and severities that forced many others to seek refuge and liberty in the New World. He married, raised a family and had numerous grandchildren. Finally, in 1816, the year after the Battle of Waterloo and the fall of Napoleon, he called a gathering of his sons and daughters and their wives and husbands, and solemnly announced that he was not going to stand for conditions any more. He was going to start for America, he informed them, and start life over again. Those who so desired might accompany him.

They all decided to go with him.

Two years later Lachlan and his sons and daughters landed on Cape Breton Island and made their way to Washabuckt and settled on the free land available there.

They were probably attracted by the scenery of the Bras d'Or Lakes as much as anything else, for it resembles that of the Scottish Highlands. Besides this, Washabuckt gave them a chance to live the amphibious kind of life that they had known in Barra, for they could fish in the salt waters of the Lake as well as cultivate the land. There were great differences, however, for Washabuckt was covered with forests, while few trees grow in windswept, bleak Barra, and the winters were longer and colder. They were not accustomed to the ice of the lakes and the heavy snows. So there were many troublesome and severe adjustments to make.

The first homes were made from logs cut from the abundant forests and built just inland from the shore of the Lake. Then they set out to clear the forests so that they might raise crops of potatoes, oats and barley. These with the fish from the Lake and the game from the forest would feed them. Later they got cattle and horses.

The first years and especially the first winter were difficult. Some of them ran out of food. Those that had food shared it, but there was not enough to go around. In those trying days my great-grandfather left home one morning and walked across the trackless ice of the lakes and the roadless snow-bound country sixty miles to Sydney. There he spent the night. Next morning he bought a 100-pound bag of oatmeal, put it on his shoulder and walked back the sixty miles home so that his family could eat.

These MacNeils and MacLeans were not long in hewing their farms out of the wilderness. They built permanent homes and barns. They built roads. In a few years they had a thriving and comfortable community. It had not changed much when I arrived at the home of my Grandfather, for Washabuckt, like Barra, was isolated from the pulsing drive of modern progress.

Lachlan MacLean lived on for twenty-four years in the New World. He had the satisfaction of seeing his sons and daughters and his grandchildren and great-grandchildren thriving in their new homes on their new farms, and if these homes were primitive according to modern ideas in each lived a happy family. He died full of years and honors at the venerable age of 114, and was buried in the local graveyard, which he, himself, had presented to the community. One hundred years later memorial services were held at his grave and nearly 1000 of his descendants gathered to do him honor. These did not include all his descendants, for many others were scattered over the face of the American continent.

CHAPTER THREE

Life in Washabuckt

ALL THE ORIGINAL Washabuckt settlers but one had died when I arrived there, but their sons and daughters were still tilling its soil and fishing in its waters; and for the most part they continued the traditions of their fathers and their way of life, for it was all they knew. Civilization had gone forward with a rush elsewhere, but not in Washabuckt. There the people lived as they had lived, and that means that they lived much as their predecessors had lived in Barra. They had made some adjustments, but these left their basic way of life unaffected.

They all spoke Gaelic, both in the home and out of it. Some of the older people, especially the women, spoke nothing else. Those who did speak English did so with a strong Gaelic accent and intonation and with an admixture of Gaelic words. They also used English words in their Gaelic, mostly words for the new things like stoves, matches, wagons and tools for the farm and utensils for the home, for Gaelic was a dead tongue and there was no way of coining new words. School courses were taught in English, but in earlier days English itself had to be learned as an alien tongue.

It seemed natural and right that Gaelic should be

spoken. Certainly Washabuckt without Gaelic would not be Washabuckt. It had centuries of tradition and usage behind it and it embodied a colorful and mystical culture.

Gaelic was and remains an expressive and flexible language, harsh to the unaccustomed ear but beautiful to one who loves it. It allowed shades of meaning that could not be carried over into English and abounded in onomatopes that made speaking a joy and ordinary conversation a display of wit. It was a grand language in which to curse, for it provided a range of denunciation and damnation that was at once alarming and magnificent; and these imaginative Scots made the most of its many opportunities, with results that had to be heard and understood to be appreciated. There were even different forms and codes of profanity for men and women, and one sex never had to impinge on the expressions of the other to give proper vent to its feelings. Gaelic was also a grand language in which to pray, for it had an intimacy and a depth of devotion that no other language can approach. The good people of Washabuckt were great cursers and great prayers, moving from one mood to another with ease and dexterity, as each came quite naturally to them.

Being a child I was not long in learning Gaelic and I was soon so adept at it that I forgot much of my English, although for a time I spoke a jargon that was neither English nor Gaelic. My Grandfather encouraged my early efforts, and even taught me to read out of his Gaelic songbooks. Later at school and at college I learned to read Gaelic, and made some acquaintance with its literature.

One of the things I soon learned was that all individuals had two names, and that one did not necessarily bear any relationship to the other. All men and women had, of course, a legal name, usually the anglicized form of the family or clan name, such as MacNeil, MacLean, MacKinnon, MacDonald, McDougall, McIver or McAulay, all of which were represented in our neighborhood, but this name was only used on legal documents, for addressing mail, and for voting. Besides this every one, with no exception, had an intimate neighborly name, by which he or she was known in Washabuckt and nearby communities. Almost always it was a Gaelic name, although sometimes it might be mixed up with English names and forms. The individual was not always addressed by this name, but he or she was identified by it.

These intimate, neighborhood names might come from the individual's size or color, occupation or locality, father or grandfather, from some personal peculiarity, or for no reason at all. In some cases it came from the mother or grandmother when one or the other was a dominant personality or simply a widow. These intimate names persist until the present and would make an interesting study in nomenclature, for they indicate how most people came by their names. In the outside world these names have become frozen into legal forms, while in Washabuckt they remained in a state of flux and confusion. Such nomenclature has been a widespread characteristic of Scottish and Irish Gaelic-speaking people. Perhaps it would be more correct to state that it is a Gaelic-speaking habit.

Thus a man in Washabuckt might be known as Big Dan the Piper. This would mean that at one time he was big, perhaps as a child in comparison with other children, as many men were named "Big" who were not so big, and that he himself, his father or his grandfather played the bagpipes. Another might be known as Red Rory the Banker. This would mean that Rory had red hair and possibly a red beard, but it would not mean that he owned or worked in a bank, for there was none in Washabuckt and little to put into one, but that he or one of his predecessors had fished on the Grand Banks, off the coast of Newfoundland. Still another might be known as Pale Paul the Ghost, which most likely would indicate that he was blond and that at one time he had told a tall story of an encounter with a ghost. There was no limit to the range of such names. All of them were picturesque and descriptive, although many of them were satiric, because no one could put bounds on the imaginative humor of these Scots. All of these Gaelic names poured off the tongue with the soft, sweet, gurgling, guttural music of a woodland brook. Translated into English such names lose much of their color and euphony and all of their alliteration and rhythm.

A few individuals resented their Gaelic names, but for the most part they were accepted with good grace as the common practice of the community and the usage of the ages.

The majority of names, however, were based on the names of the individual's father and grandfather, and show how the Scottish clans came by their names. For instance my Grandfather was known as Michael Eoin, which had its origin in the fact that his own given name was Michael and that of his father Eoin, or John. In turn my father was known as John Michael Eoin, his given name being John, and this being added to the neighborhood name of his father. Some of these names were also colorful and expressive in Gaelic. A list of them could be compiled that would rival the melodious flow of the names of the ships in Homer's Greek.

Gaelic lent itself to the natural bent of the people for music and poetry. For the real Scots, those from the Highlands and the Islands of Scotland (not those from the Lowlands) are a dreamy, poetical, mystical people and not at all the hard, sharp, thrifty, practical people modern Americans think them.

LIFE IN WASHABUCKT was simple and innocent and its tempo was sluggish. The men tilled their unproductive farms with the maximum of physical effort and

the minimum of machinery, fished in the waters of the
Lake, and hunted and cut wood in the forests; but their
work was mostly seasonal, so they never worked hard
for long. The work of the women never ended, however.
They did all the work of the home and they helped also
in the fields. Besides the cooking and baking, the cleaning and the washing, they milked the cows, fed the poultry, planted and hoed the potatoes, raked the hay; and
when they had nothing else to do they sheared the sheep,
washed the wool, spun it into yarn and knitted or wove it
and made the clothing for the family.

All the younger men and women found ample time
for visiting their neighbors and the nearby villages and
for attending the numerous frolics or dances—especially
during the long winters.

There was a sharp cleavage between the duties of the
sexes and their work, and those of one did not do those
of the other. That native of Washabuckt was always
astounded when abroad to find men waiting on tables or
cooking and washing dishes in hotels and restaurants, for
these he considered the prerogatives as well as the duties
of women, and his opinion of men that would do such
things cannot be recorded in polite language. Moreover,
he was not timid in expressing this opinion, and, but for
the fact that it was generally expressed in Gaelic and
hence unintelligible to the offenders of the Washabuckt
code, might have started many a fracas, which of course
would have been welcomed by the Washabuckter.

Washabuckt homes were in keeping with the life of
the people. They were built for utility and not for beauty.
They offered few comforts and no modern convenienc-
es. Most of them were story-and-a-half frame structures,
some white-washed, usually unfinished on the ground
floor except for board partitions and completely unfinished in the attic except for the floor. The largest and
principal room was always the kitchen and in it centered

all family and most social activities. Some homes had a dining room and most a parlor but these were usually reserved for important events, such as a dance or the visit of the parish priest.

A huge, black, crude, wood-burning iron stove on legs, with an ungainly oven perched upon it, dominated the kitchen and served for cooking the meals for the family and the feed for the stock, and for heating the home. There was always a black steaming and whistling iron kettle sitting on the stove, and a stack of cut firewood beside it. On winter nights the family sat around the stove, the men placing their stockinged feet upon it, so that the women had to step over or around them to place pots on the stove or pans in the oven.

Windows were generally nailed fast when the house was built and never opened, but chill blasts blew through the rooms whenever a door was opened. Further to seal the home eelgrass was gathered on the shores of the Lake in the fall and piled around its foundations, remaining there until spring when it was spread on the fields for fertilizer.

The homes were lighted at night by kerosene lamps, sometimes supplemented by crude, homemade candles made from mutton tallow. The polish of the lamp globes, an art in itself, told of the industry and efficiency of the housewife.

All the water for the home was brought in buckets from a nearby well, although some might be obtained by melting snow or catching rainwater from the roof. Often it would be necessary to break the ice on the buckets to get a drink, or water for a wash.

The furniture was simple, consisting of wooden chairs, or benches, a couple of tables, beds for the family, and the always present spinning wheel. Wooden chests, and sometimes wooden boxes obtained with the purchase of merchandise, served as bureaus, storage for valuables, and as extra seats.

Much was made of little, and everything served a purpose.

Of sanitary facilities there were none in the home, and rarely any outside of it but what nature itself provided. Of course there was the lake for bathing in the summer months and the abundant forests for still more intimate and private personal requirements. The natives of Washabuckt did not miss sanitary facilities or think them necessary, for their ancestors had survived in good health and vigor for centuries without bathrooms and lavatories. Moreover, many of them, an unusually high percentage, had reached a venerable old age. As men and women they felt sufficient unto themselves and did not court the frills and artifices, the luxuries and mechanics, of modern civilization. They knew that there were such things but they looked with contempt upon such effete influences. True, outside progress, the excrescences of the alien culture, intruded at times, and some individuals gave way to them for a time, but most of them soon returned to Washabuckt norms.

Take for instance the sad case of Little Rory Donald Dhu. Rory had a daughter who some years before had gone to Boston, often known in Cape Breton as the Boston States. Boston in those days was the Valhalla of all ambitious Washabuckt boys and girls who ventured out into the world to better themselves. Many of them prospered. Rory's daughter did well by herself, and she married a lawyer with a large practice and an ample income. After some years of happy married life, she decided that it was safe to take her high-toned husband to visit her father and mother. In due time they took up residence with Little Rory.

They were not long on Rory's farm before the daughter had occasion to use a bathroom only to confirm what she already knew—that Rory had no bathroom and nothing else to take its place. So she gave her father ten dollars and told him to buy some lumber and build a backhouse.

Rory got the lumber; the lawyer-husband drew the design and supervised the work; and the backhouse was built. It was quite pretentious for Washabuckt. It was even rumored that it was a three-holer. It was well patronized for the rest of the summer.

Next summer the daughter and her husband visited Rory again, for once you get to know Washabuckt its lure is irresistible. They were not long back when the daughter had occasion to visit the backhouse, only to find that it had vanished. There was not a trace of it anywhere on the farm.

The daughter set out to seek an explanation from Little Rory. She found him killing potato bugs in a field some distance from the house.

"What happened to the backhouse?" she demanded.

"The backhouse!" he replied, reluctantly. "Oh, yes, I tore it down."

"Why?" she insisted.

"I had my reasons."

"What reasons?"

"They were good reasons."

"I must know your reasons. After all it was my backhouse. It was my property."

"Well, if you must know you must know," Rory confessed; "the neighbors used to point at me and say, 'There goes proud Rory what does it in a box.'"

What Little Rory Donald Dhu did not tell his daughter was that he now had a new Washabuckt name. Translated into polite English it was "Little Rory the Backhouse," which was frequently abridged into "The Backhouse."

Then again there was the experience of Holy Angus, one of the admitted leaders of the community, a man of dignified mien, extensive learning and solemn wisdom. The parish priest always stayed at Angus's home when he came to Washabuckt on parochial visits, as there were at that time no church and no rectory to receive him. All the neighbors, except the three Protestant families, would gather into Angus's home for their spiritual consolation.

After the long, hard day and a hearty supper the priest and Holy Angus would sit by the stove in the kitchen and talk things over. They would discuss the affairs of the countryside and of the world as they looked from Cape Breton.

On one such night the priest made his usual nightly visit to a nearby clump of trees before retiring. It was a cold, rainy, windy night, and it evidently set the good old priest thinking, for on his return to the house and the fireside he addressed Angus to this effect:

"Conditions in Washabuckt are entirely too primitive. As one of the local leaders you should set a good example in progress. Civilized people do not expose themselves to the winds and the rain this way. Instead they have a backhouse. It does not cost much to build a backhouse; and one is easy to build. First you dig a pit about six feet deep. Then you build a house over it, say about four feet by six and high enough for a grown man to stand up in it. You put a floor over one-half of it and over the other half you place a seat. You make the seat by nailing two wide boards together at right angles; one makes the back of the seat, and in the other you cut a hole. You place the seat over the pit. That's all there is to it."

Some months later when the priest made a return visit Holy Angus was in high spirits, for he had followed the priest's instruction to the letter. When it came time to retire, he gave the priest a lighted lantern and pointed proudly to the backhouse. It had been reserved for his sole use. The priest made his way to the backhouse. He found that Angus had done his work well. Then he stepped inside, and there he found also that Angus had followed directions. Everything was complete; Angus had placed the seat made from the two boards over the pit and made the hole as ordered. The hole, however, was a one-inch auger hole.

The structure was known henceforth in Washabuckt as the "Kirk."

As bathrooms were unknown the Washabuckt ladies naturally had to get along without boudoirs and all the facilities and artifices for beauty and charm that these require or imply. In fact cosmetics of all kinds were almost unknown. I say almost, for there were a few exceptions. The average young lady had to depend on the beauty that God gave her, enhanced perhaps by the salubrious climate, the healthy outdoor life and simple living. When she had color in her cheeks it was due to the flow of blood beneath a healthy skin. When her eyes flashed, or her lips looked like ripe cherries, or her hair dropped in golden ringlets it meant that these were part of her physical equipment. While paint and powder and lipstick and perfume had not reached Washabuckt there was plenty of soap and water; and a good scrubbing brought a glow to the skin, a sheen to the hair and a liveliness to the spirit. Artificial beauty aids were not missed much, for often they were not needed.

The ladies of Washabuckt, as of all Cape Breton, in those days cherished and sought a pale, white, translucent, alabaster skin unmarred by any tan or blemish; and great efforts were made to protect these blanched complexions from the summer sun. Freckles were abhorred and avoided like sin, for sad indeed was the lot of the gay young lady whose face was sprinkled with them. The men did not notice them much, but the women did, and even in Washabuckt that was something to cause grave concern.

Freckles led to a near tragedy in the home of my Grandfather. A young lady from the United States was a visitor one summer. With her she brought one of the

Michael MacNeil (Neil MacNeil's grandfather—his father's father) and John A. MacNeil (Neil's father, 1859-1913), to whom Neil dedicated *The Highland Heart in Nova Scotia*: "This book is affectionately dedicated to the memory of my Father, who would have liked it; and of my Grandfather—who certainly wouldn't."

John Murdoch MacNeil (born 1895; killed in action June 10, 1916), Lucy MacNeil Hayes (1894-1995), and Neil Francis MacNeil (1891-1969). John Murdoch (9), Lucy (10), and Neil (13) were photographed in Sydney, Cape Breton, in 1904.

Above, Neil as a baby.
Right, Neil at two years of age.

Neil F. in the
United States Army

Neil MacNeil and his wife
Elizabeth Quinn MacNeil
in the 1950s

Neil MacNeil at his desk in the managing editor's bullpen
at *The New York Times* in the 1940s

June 1947, St. Francis Xavier College: Neil MacNeil received an honorary
degree and made the commencement speech. Left to right: Neil MacNeil;
Father Rankin of Iona; Joseph MacNeil, youngest brother of Neil's father
John A.; and Father Nicholson, president of the College.

**Captain Alex MacLean—
known in Jack London's
novel as the "Sea Wolf"**

**Copper Jack
(see page 61)**

**Above left: John A. MacNeil (1838-1897), Neil MacNeil's mother's father.
Right: "The Millionaire," Neil MacNeil's great-uncle Neil McNeil (1842-1921).**

Neil MacNeil, appearing with former President Herbert Hoover,
when Hoover testified on the
presidency in 1956 before a U.S.
Senate sub-committee chaired
by Senator John F. Kennedy.

magazines published for ladies. This particular magazine was modest enough of itself, for it dealt mostly with the latest styles, with articles on food and on managing children; but it also contained advertisements. One of these advertisements extolled a cure for freckles, a positive cure, and all for one dollar.

It so happened that this young lady and a young female relative of mine had freckles—a few that I had not noticed but which worried them not a little. So they sent a letter to New York with a dollar, and one day, some time later, a strange package arrived by mail. There were feminine conferences over the package accompanied by giggling and whispers, and the two ladies disappeared upstairs to their own quarters to open it. They not only opened the package but they also applied the remedy to their skins.

They arose early next morning to examine themselves in their mirror. What they beheld was appalling. They were as black as Congo maidens, black as darkest midnight.

Their wails and weeping brought Grandmother to the scene. With her help they tried to wipe their complexions clean. They tried everything, including kerosene and turpentine, but that black would not wipe off. It seemed to be indelible. It seemed permanent.

Of course they could not appear downstairs or in public. It was important that Grandfather not know about it, for that would mean an explosion. Great efforts were taken to keep the affair a secret. Grandfather was told that they were ill. I and other male relatives heard the same story. Suspecting that something was amiss I appeared on the scene, and was fortunate to escape with my life. Grandmother brought them food and other necessaries, and they remained in seclusion.

Days passed into weeks while the two ladies tried desperately to resume their natural color. It was six weeks before they dared put in an appearance, and it was almost ten weeks before they were normal again.

When the blackness finally left, it took the freckles with it. It was a cure for freckles after all; but these two maidens did not write any testimonials for the new remedy.

THE PLEASURES OF THE PEOPLE of Washabuckt were in keeping with the simple, rugged outdoor life that they lived.

The men drank their Scotch whiskey straight and at a gulp. It was the only liquor they knew, and they could never obtain enough of it, although it sold for less than a dollar a bottle. They smoked black, strong plug tobacco in strong, black pipes. They liked to talk and to sing and to fight.

The women liked to visit, to gossip and to pray. They took snuff in large doses, as did some of the men; and they pretended to faint at the smell or mention of whiskey, although local gossip had it that some of them drank plenty in private.

Both men and women enjoyed dancing to the music of the fiddle and the bagpipes, always square dances, the Highland reel and the lancers, and the men would swing the women about violently and stamp the floor with their feet. Every sort of excuse was employed to have a dance, or a frolic as it was usually called, which often ended in a battle royal among the liquored men. A frolic was no place for weaklings and cowards.

Everybody, no matter how he or she croaked, loved to sing Gaelic songs at work and at play. The Washabuckter would burst into song with or without any excuse. These Gaelic songs had a strong melodic line and many of them had a rousing chorus. Men would swing an ax or a scythe to the rhythm of a swinging song. Women would sing as they rubbed the family wash in a running brook or busied themselves about the home.

They had learned what modern industry is only now learning, that music makes work easier. When two or more were at the same task it was customary for one to sing the verses of the song and for the others to join in the chorus. Some of these songs rambled on verse after verse for a half-hour or so and were a good test of memory. They almost never sang English songs, for to the Gaelic-trained ear these seemed inept and dull.

The Washabuckters brought these Gaelic songs with them from Barra and one generation taught them to the next as had been done for centuries in the old country. Most songs told a story of the life of the Scots, of their loves and lovemaking, of their hunting in the glens, of their glories on the battlefields. Some families had bound collections of Gaelic songs, and one of the reasons why they wanted to read Gaelic was that they could learn their songs. The local community was not without its bards, however, who sang of the local happenings, and who were held in something approaching awe and fear. The Washabuckter dreaded nothing more in life than being the butt of the satire of one of the local bards, for that indeed would be difficult to live down; that kind of immortality he did not relish.

The people of Washabuckt did almost no formal entertaining. One was almost never invited to visit a home except to attend a dance or a frolic. Good neighbors were expected to visit their friends and they did at all hours of the day, and especially at night, but no invitations were sent out. A family was always "at home," and if the visitor found the housewife or the man of the house at work that was only to be expected and the visitor sat and talked just the same or joined in the labors. No one was ever invited to dinner or supper. If one dropped in at mealtime he or she was welcome to the meal that the family was about to eat and nothing extra was provided and there was no attempt at show.

The Washabuckters ate to live and did not waste any time at it. Their food was what their farms, the forest and the Lake provided. The cooking was simple but adequate. These people worked hard and they had lusty appetites and good digestions. They loved confections and culinary delicacies as other people do, but these were rare, and for the most part the diet was coarse—boiled meats or fish, potatoes, turnips, eggs, milk and butter or molasses. They did not know coffee but they loved tea and this with hot soda bread and butter was usually served to casual visitors. The tropical fruits and other exotic foods they did not know, and they would probably not have known what to do with them.

There was such an experience when Crooked Sandy's daughter got married. Up to this time this was the nearest thing to a feast that Washabuckt had ever known. Sandy was strong on show and something of a braggart, so when a relative in the Boston States sent a cured ham to grace the occasion, Sandy announced it to the neighborhood and promised all and sundry a special treat. The more curious dropped in to look at the ham and to feel it, and there was much speculation as to how one would eat it. Sandy informed them that he knew all about hams and told them not to worry about it.

On the wedding day the raw ham was brought in on a platter. Sandy poured some cider vinegar over it, sliced it with a carving knife and passed around chunks of it on plates. The guests had difficulty in eating the raw ham, but, not wanting to display ignorance in public, made the best of it. It was the subject of gossip for years afterwards; and there was no rush to get any more hams.

This wedding was not typical of Washabuckt, and lest one get a false impression I shall give a few details of the wedding of Black Hector's daughter. Hector sported the grandest crop of black whiskers for miles about but was a simple and modest man for all that. His daughter was a charming lass, and well deserved all Hector could do for her.

The wedding party drove the nine miles by horse and buggy from Washabuckt to the church at Iona for the ceremony. All the persons directly concerned, including Hector, went fasting, for there was to be a nuptial mass and communion, and after the long ceremony they had to drive the nine miles back to Hector's home for the wedding feast. This was customary.

In each buggy was at least one bottle of whiskey. Some of the guests took a swig or two of the liquor on the way to the church, but of course none of the principals broke the fast. After the ceremony it was different and the bottles were emptied on the long, slow but gay drive home amid laughter, cheers and singing. By the time they were approaching Hector's house the merriment was all that could be expected or desired.

Meanwhile the older women of the family and their women friends were preparing the wedding dinner, for that it was to be. A dozen women busied themselves about the setting of the tables with the borrowed dishes and cutlery, and a dozen more busied themselves about the kitchen. One table was stacked with loaves of bread and cakes. But the stove dominated the scene: on it sat a half-dozen bubbling and steaming pots.

As soon as the wedding party returned, Black Hector staggered into the kitchen. He pushed two or three women aside and walked up to the stove. He lifted the lid off one of the pots.

"If it's going to be a wedding, let it be a wedding," says he; "put another herrin' in the pot."

A grand time was had by all.

GRANDMOTHER DID MAKE two attempts to introduce the use of napkins into Washabuckt, simply because Father had made her a present of two dozen; but the results each time were disastrous, and the attempts were not repeated.

The first attempt was one time Holy Angus was present for supper. Without a word to anybody Grandmother put a folded napkin beside each plate at the table. Angus was halfway through the meal before he noticed it. Evidently it worried him a bit, for he would gaze at it suspiciously and then look around the table. As the others had their napkins in their laps and thus out of sight, he could get no guidance from them.

Finally, he picked up the napkin with an air of determination, and blew his nose into it in a series of blasts and snorts that sounded like Gabriel's trumpet.

The second attempt to bring the more delicate amenities of life to Washabuckt was during a visit by Allen Donald the Cobbler. Allen was a great talker and Grandfather enjoyed his visits. Grandmother served the two of them tea in the kitchen. After handing them the tea and soda bread she silently slipped what would now be called a cocktail napkin into Allen's lap. It was a dainty thing of Irish linen edged with lace. Allen was arguing some point so ardently that he did not see her do so.

Some minutes later, in taking a sip from the cup of tea, Allen's eyes glanced downward and noticed the white cloth in his lap. He thought it was his shirt-tail sticking out. No man was ever more embarrassed. He fidgeted about for some minutes awaiting his chance, and when he thought no one was looking stuffed in the napkin into his trousers. Then he made his excuses and left abruptly. That was the last Grandmother saw of her dainty napkin.

Then again there was the time Father gave Grandmother a present of some flat silverware from his Boston home. Grandfather found the silver knives too dull and took them out to the barn to sharpen them on the grindstone. He was enraged when he could not get them to take a sharp edge. By the time he was through with them he had ground most of the silver off the blades and they were queer-looking weapons. However, they were used at table for company for years afterwards, and served a useful purpose for Grandfather, as they gave him a topic of conversation. He would expatiate on the stupidity of people, like the Yankees, who would make knives of silver when there was plenty of steel in the world. He placed the silver knives in the same class as the wooden nutmegs of Connecticut.

Probably the most revealing fact of life in Washabuckt was that no one locked a door and that you entered any home without knocking. Some of the doors had wooden latches that could be turned to prevent the door being opened from the outside; but these were there for the windy weather and not to shut out the neighbors or the few straggling strangers that entered the community. There were no locks because there was nothing to fear. Burglary and robbery were unknown, and so also were sex crimes and other crimes of violence. Life was innocent as well as simple. At heart the people were clean and honest. The visiting neighbor was always welcome, for he always came through friendship and not to do injury.

CHAPTER FOUR

A Free and Hardy People

THE PEOPLE OF WASHABUCKT, especially the older people, had a profound wisdom that is difficult to explain and a philosophy that is not easy to grasp. They knew little of the history and sciences of the world; they knew almost nothing of literature and culture; they knew still less of the formal philosophies and theologies: yet in their own way they knew more than most learned savants know, for they understood nature in its many and varied moods.

They were content with little, and thus they had the deepest secret of life. They were, of course, unconscious of it.

This is often true of people who live close to nature; and in Washabuckt the people not only toiled on the soil, but they walked in the forests, and fished in the waters of the sea. They could fend for themselves as could the flowers in the meadow, the fox in the brakes, and the trout in the deep pools. Such people seem to have a special endowment from the God of creation, who cares for his own. They have a calm that the people of the city can seldom acquire, a simplicity that is close to the sublime, a fortitude that belittles the adversities of life. These are elements of true greatness that formal education cannot give, nor money buy.

The citizen of the teeming metropolis moves in his pride and scorns his rustic neighbor. Look at him: he is nervous, bored, tired, irritable, rushing about to get nowhere. He has a terrifying impatience with himself and most everything else. He needs external amusements to crowd out each moment of leisure, and stimulants to live out each day. He rarely knows the blessings of solitude. He wears a veneer of culture, put on like cosmetics from the drugstore. He places a cash value on everything and approaches most things with the thought: "What is in it for me?" Often he is not a pleasant companion, nor a good neighbor. Most of the troubles of this troubled world are born in its cities and fostered in their festering sores. The rustic takes time to be calm. He has a truer sense of values.

True freedom from want is only enjoyed by those who desire nothing material. Most civilized persons are chained to their worldly possessions as the dog is chained to his kennel. Human greed is basically the cause of most human troubles.

Thus the religious who take vows of poverty, chastity, and obedience are probably the only truly free persons living; in denying the world and its goods, they gain all that is worth while, in their case time to contemplate God. This explains why mighty kings have turned in disgust from the world and its pomp and retired to monasteries. This is also why the tramp on the highway is both free and happy. It explains why there is something of the tramp or the gypsy in all of us, especially the more civilized among us. We crave for release from the bondage imposed by position and possessions.

Thus also the child is free, free to dream and free to follow every whim. Who does not look back with nostalgia to the carefree days of youth, even when that youth was somewhat harsh and sordid? No matter what else it was, it was a time when we were not laden with the cares and trials of life and we could mix dreams with reality. No wonder our youth takes on glamour as the years overtake us. What great man would not exchange his wealth and honors for a few years of new youth when he could again spare time to enjoy himself and have a boundless capacity for doing so?

The people of Washabuckt had few desires and few inhibitions. They were not burdened with worldly goods, and the majority of them would have been embarrassed with more than they had. They enjoyed the little, simple things in life and as these were at hand and easy to grasp they had large opportunity for enjoyment. They always had food and shelter and clothes, so there was little to worry about. There was never such a thing as a nervous breakdown or a heart attack. They had time to take things easy and they never thought of retiring from work. The pace of life was slow and there was little change except that brought by the cycle of the seasons. Men and women went on living from youth to venerable old age never wealthy and never really poor, seldom troubled and never released from work.

These Washabuckt people were so free that they never gave freedom a thought. In fact they were so free themselves that they could not conceive of any one who was not free. Freedom does not come from charters or constitutions; it comes from the spirit of such people, who are free because they act free and could not accept restraint or oppression. The people who talk much about freedom, it seems to me, do so because they know little about it. You never discuss breathing or argue about your rights to do so because there is an abundance of air and you can help yourself to all you want of it without denying your neighbor all he also wants of it. So it was with freedom; it is so natural to free people that they take it without thinking about it.

In Washabuckt there were no imposed laws, no agencies of government, no visible oppressors, few of the trappings of civilization. Men and women went about their daily tasks and amusements without any idea of political or economic security. They never turned to government for anything, certainly not for their right to live out their lives as they wanted to live them. They knew nothing of the Magna Charta, constitutional law, or such things as a Declaration of Independence and the long fight for human liberty. Only the people of a poor, simple, rural community, one where the people own the land, can know such freedom.

I have known many of the leaders of the world of our time and numerous men of wealth but I have yet to meet one of either class who was happy or free. Great responsibilities or huge possessions, sometimes both, so burdened their lives and so occupied their time that they could not lead happy lives, and often could not spare time to love their own families. Few of them could be calm or think things through, for they were rushed, irritable, nervous, afraid and dissatisfied with themselves and with things in general. Often they had broken their health in their drive for position or for wealth, and could not be happy if they had the time and the chance. Almost without exception they dreaded the prospect of losing their honors or their money. They did not know how to live and they were afraid to die. They had won their struggle for wealth or position at tremendous cost, only to have it turn to dust in their hands. One of the saddest things in life is the celebrity seeking the peace that the world denies to him.

THE PEOPLE OF WASHABUCKT were proud, as all Scottish people are proud; and yet they were humble. Burns understood this when he wrote of Highland pride and Highland cold and hunger. These transplanted Scots had pride of name and pride of race. They admitted no superiors and were not awed by worldly pomp and wealth. It was the kind of pride that is above and beyond grand mansions, liveried servants, position, and adulation. They bore themselves with dignity and did not feel that honest, menial work was degrading. Was not Christ a carpenter? They recognized that a man must earn his bread by the sweat of his brow, and they felt that work was work and that it elevated rather than lowered man in the presence of his neighbor and his God.

It would not do to question the basis of this Scottish pride, as these people were proud without knowing it. Perhaps it was due to the Clan system, which for centuries cultivated the Clansman's pride in his family and Clan. Yet they were easy to offend, and quick to strike. The outsider might consider this quixotic and amusing; but there it was. He could have a fight in the flick of an eyelid by doubting it. Few did.

They had their mean traits too and the worst of these was their intense jealousy of their neighbors. So long as one conformed to local norms all was well; but when one "put on airs" or assumed superiority of position or education the scorn and wrath of the community would devour him. They did not tolerate the man or the woman who tried to rise above them. They especially resented the native returning to Washabuckt after years in the United States with money in his pockets and tales of strange places and stranger doings.

This jealousy led to trouble and even to feuds that lasted for decades. The conformist would pick an argument or a fight with the nonconformist and it would be the talk of the community for months with all the sympathy going to the former. My Father often encountered this disagreeable trait among his boyhood friends who could not forgive him his success, which was admitted even in Washabuckt, but no one dared pick a fight with

Father, for he could deal with the best of them, as they well knew. He enjoyed their envy, and told them so.

As is usually the case, this jealousy was accompanied by an overwhelming curiosity about their neighbors. What every one did, wore, bought, sold, planted, reaped, built, planned, ate, suffered, loved and despised were subject to community inquiry and comment, favorable and unfavorable. Moreover, every activity was exaggerated or belittled as it suited the gossiper. The privacy of the individual was no more respected there than it is in the yellow journals of the American metropolis, or anywhere else for that matter. A sweet morsel of scandal was relished by all, and would pass over the countryside with the speed of a modern radio broadcast. Gossip was at all times a favorite occupation and entertainment.

This insatiable curiosity was evident everywhere and on all occasions, but never more so than when you drove in a horse and carriage along the country roads. There were no automobiles in those days, so you drove at a speed ranging from five to nine miles an hour. The latter speed would mean cruelty to your horse, and leave a wave of scandal in your wake. Your progress was never so fast that it did not give ample time for neighborly curiosity.

Men and women would stop work in the fields to gaze unabashed at you, and stand gazing so long as you remained in sight. Faces young and old, male and female, would appear in the windows of the homes. If they did not recognize you. There would be inquiries for days until the mystery was dissolved. If any person was on the road or working near it, you were expected in courtesy to stop to pass the time of day with him, whether you knew him or not. Persons would inquire where you were going and why and seek other pertinent information. Later they could report what you wore, the state of your health, how your horse and rig looked, and hazard a guess as to the money in your pocket. Nothing escaped them.

If perchance they did not recognize you, they would without doubt identify the horse and carriage, and could thus tell whence you came and where you were going and what you were about. They were experts in observation and deduction.

Then there were the road detectives, the men and women who could tell who had passed along the rocky, rain-ditched dirt road during the day by the tracks left by the horse and carriage. This was sometimes difficult for them during the summer months when the roads were dusty but easy after a shower which left the roads damp. They seldom failed. In fact they had brought this form of detection to a fine art. They would have shamed Sherlock Holmes or Arsène Lupin.

There was one young man in Washabuckt in my time who was the champion at this kind of thing. On examination of the tracks he could identify every horse and its owner in a radius of ten miles. I was among his most ardent admirers and often made him perform just to see him do it. He never let me in to all his secrets but he did disclose some of them. It seems that different horses have variations in the shape of their hoofs and how they place those hoofs on the road. Not all horseshoes are made or shaped alike. And there is a wide variation in the length of the horse's pace. Then there were differences in the shape of the carriage wheels, of the width of the rims, of the alignment of the front and the rear wheels. He studied these in combinations of horses and carriage, and with the help of a good memory and great talent made his finding. He was so accurate that his testimony could have been accepted in a court of law.

I felt that these extraordinary talents of his were wasted in Washabuckt and I expected important things of him when he later made his way to Boston. He became the night watchman at a warehouse, and that was the last I heard of him. It seems, however, that he never did get an opportunity to use his extraordinary ability, for if he had he would have been famous in no time. But that is the way life is: we seldom get the chance to do the things for which we are best fitted and which bring us the most pleasure.

Along with this intense curiosity about one's neighbors went an equal reluctance on the part of each of those neighbors to reveal anything personal to inquirers. This was especially true with strangers, who were viewed with suspicion anyway. The native of Washabuckt would go to great lengths to hide trivial affairs which were bound to be known later. They seemed to enjoy prolonging the agony of the curious as long as possible. In this respect it was a form of sadism. "Face" was as important in Washabuckt as it ever was in the Orient, and woe to the person who insisted on asking the embarrassing question. It were better that he had never heard of Cape Breton.

There were ways of doing it, however; and it was interesting to watch the play of wits as one curious Washabuckter would extract data from another equally determined not to give up the information sought. This developed a sort of circumlocution, a kind of "beating about the bush," in which one implied more or meant less than one said. This eagerness to know on the one side and the desire to hide on the other brought about many tests of wit.

One of these was between my grandfather and Ronald Black Murdoch. Of this I was a witness.

Grandfather and I were driving to Upper Washabuckt on business. When we reached Ronald's farm we found Ronald and a hired man working in a field beside the road. They had a pile of scantling and lumber and were obviously erecting a building of some sort. Judging by the foundation, which was partly laid, it was to be a structure of considerable size. What it was to be could not be discovered from the evidence. Grandfather's curiosity was aroused.

We stopped the horse and carriage by the roadside, as was the custom, and Ronald left his work and came to the roadside to pass the time of day with us, which was the proper thing to do, for a neighbor in Washabuckt was always more important than any work that was to be done. After they had expressed the usual banalities about the state of their health and about the weather, Grandfather started the quest with an oblique attack.

"That's a good pile of lumber you have, Ronald," he said hopefully, but knowing full well that he would not get much information.

"That it is," responded Ronald, revealing exactly nothing.

"I can see you have quite a bit of scantling," put in Grandfather.

"That I have," retorted Ronald and Grandfather was just where he had begun.

"It would make a good-sized building, it would," continued Grandfather, coming closer to the real subject.

"Indeed and it would," was Ronald's answer.

The conversation went on in this manner for a full fifteen minutes, much like a prosecuting attorney trying to get a confession from a known murderer. Grandfather would never ask the improper question, and Ronald would not surrender the information he knew Grandfather wanted. It was clear to me that Grandfather was getting the better of the trail of wits, for he was far abler intellectually and more adroit, but Ronald dodged question after question, which seemed silly to me, for the building would be completed in a few days and the whole neighborhood would know all about it and its purposes.

Finally Grandfather got more aggressive, yet without violating the local code, and when Ronald found himself being trapped, he remarked with some satire:

"Well, if you must know, Michael Eoin, you must know. It is going to be a backhouse."

"Well, well, well," replied Grandfather slowly and deliberately, looking over the lumber and the foundation, "so it is going to be a backhouse! It will be large as backhouses go; but then you will not be long in filling it."

With that he said "Giddap" to the horse and we continued on our way to Upper Washabuckt. When built, the structure turned out to be a hay barn.

Then there was the time that Holy Angus got the better of the prosecuting attorney in the trial at Baddeck, the nearby village and county seat. The crime was not serious and it did not concern Angus or any of his kin, so the Crown called Angus as a friendly witness. All went well until the attorney tried to get Angus to be more specific than Angus wanted to be. He then discovered that Holy Angus was a tough proposition.

Angus dodged every question that the attorney asked. No matter how he tried to pin Angus down to exact information, Angus found some evasion. The attorney appealed to the court and the court admonished Angus, but it was all the same. It was not that Angus did not answer; he did. In fact he gave the correct answer to every question. The trouble was that the answer told nothing, and the trial was getting nowhere.

In desperation the attorney displayed a map of Washabuckt which was intended to give the court some idea of the location of the crime and the distance to other pertinent places in the community. Returning to Angus and indicating places on the map he asked:

"How far is it from this point to this?"

"I never surveyed it," replied Angus.

"Well, how far is it as the crow flies?"

"I never was a crow," retorted Angus.

Here the court adjourned for the day, and when it was resumed Angus was not recalled to the witness stand.

THESE PEOPLE had little ambition beyond making a living. That done, they were willing to let other people live their own lives in their own way. They were individualists with a high regard for individual rights. They accepted the religion of their fathers with simple faith and without question, and while they did not like the religions of others it never occurred to them to interfere with their practice of them. In politics they were intense during elections, which were fought on personalities mostly, but here again they had no idea of interfering with the right of their opponents to have a contrary opinion and to vote as they wished. They accepted defeat at the polls without rancor. Their ideas did not go much further than the problems of making a livelihood on their own land and raising a family.

The young men and women who did not like the prospects that Washabuckt had to offer, and there were usually some in each of their large families, migrated to the United States, where some of them made good and others fared no better than they would have at home. Those who left were expected to send money to the folks on the farm, and often did. Those who remained in Washabuckt did so from choice and not because they were less competent or less talented. They were simply contented to live as their ancestors had lived and to accept what Washabuckt had to offer, which in many ways was considerable.

The great majority of the people who remained in Washabuckt and lived out their lives there seldom, if ever, left the immediate community, which might be considered to include Iona, nine miles away, which had a railroad station and the church, Baddeck, the county seat, a few miles across the lake, where much of the marketing and trading and all of the legal work was done, and Washabuckt Bridge, five miles from Grandfather's farm, at the upper end of Upper Washabuckt, which had two general stores and a sawmill. So the community could be described as a triangle, with each side about ten miles in length. Few persons ventured as far as Sydney, sixty miles away and the largest city in Cape Breton, and almost none to Halifax, one hundred and fifty miles away, the capital of Nova Scotia. Contacts with the world outside their own community were few.

Grandfather was one of the few natives who ever went to the United States on a sightseeing trip. Father prevailed on him to visit our Boston home. This was in the 'nineties when he was in his seventies. He had three other sons in Boston and he wanted to see them too. So one summer after the crops were planted he left Washabuckt, went to Iona, boarded the train there for Halifax, where he took a boat to East Boston. His four sons met him and escorted him to our home on Meeting House Hill in Dorchester. He remained with us for about six weeks, for he had to be back in Washabuckt for the harvest.

Grandfather viewed Boston with an immense capacity for suspicion. He trusted nobody and nothing. He had heard of the city slickers, the lecherous women, the crime waves and all that is embraced in the rural conception of a modern Babylon. He had also heard of the great fires, that of London centuries before, and that of Chicago not so long before. So he was taking no chances. He insisted on sleeping on the ground floor of our three-story home, which meant that a bed had to be set up for him in the back parlor. And he would not retire for the night until all the doors had been double-locked and all the windows closed and locked. He even accepted restaurant and hotel food with grave doubts, as he had been cautioned about dope and poisoning. He did not drink alcoholic liquor in any form, which was a relief to Father.

Each night Father would see Grandfather to bed about nine o'clock and turn off the gaslight, for there was danger that the old gentleman would blow it out, and by his own act confirm his many suspicions of evil doings in the city. After that the whole house dared not move or speak, for he was a light sleeper, and he expected the house to be burglarized or burned down during the night, and every sound disturbed him. On several occasions he did get up and wander about the house in his homemade underwear, for he would not wear night clothes.

As Grandfather was undressing one night, his wallet slipped out of his pocket and dropped on the carpet. It held all his money, his return tickets, and all his papers. Father quietly picked up the wallet and slipped it into his own pocket. He bade the old man good night and left him to his slumbers.

By dawn the next morning the storm broke. The whole family was aroused and so was much of the neighborhood. Grandfather had awakened and discovered that he had been robbed. He damned Boston and all its people and all its works. He exhausted all the invective of the English language and then started into Gaelic, which in inexhaustible. He roared and cursed for two hours. He turned savagely on Father for inducing him to visit such a Hell of Iniquity and announced that he was heading back for Washabuckt at once, even if he had to walk it. This he was quite capable of doing.

Father tried to calm him, as the storm had gone even beyond what he had expected. He pleaded with him to remain at least until evening to give the police a chance to deal with the thieves. After much persuasion, Grandfather agreed to do this.

Father then left for his day's work in the city proper.

On his way he stopped at a nearby police station. There he told the captain, who was a friend of his, all about the robbery and gave him the wallet to return to Grandfather that afternoon, after a search of the house and other gestures at hunting the crooks. This the captain and his police did.

When Father returned from work that evening all was bright and beautiful. Grandfather had his wallet and all its contents. He had, of course, convincing evidence of the wickedness of the city; but he also had convincing evidence of the efficiency of its police. He was willing to concede from then on that all was not evil in Boston, as it also had capable and honest policemen to cope with its thieves and murderers. He was happy to leave it, however, and head back for Cape Breton.

On the first Sunday after Grandfather's return to the farm his old cronies for miles around gathered at his home to hear about his journey and his experiences. They sat in a great circle about the kitchen stove, and Grandmother served them tea and cakes. Grandfather was in his glory. He had the kind of audience he liked and he poured out tale after ale, one more wonderful than the other, in lurid and colorful Gaelic. He was a good storyteller and he was enjoying himself.

He told them about the street cars that ran about the streets with a pole on a wire. He told them about the piped water in the homes, with both hot and cold available by the turning of a spigot. He told them about the bathrooms, and about the gas stoves in the kitchens. The latter made Grandmother stop in her tracks and listen intently. He told them of many modern marvels, of the traffic in the streets, of the great docks with huge steel ships coming and going to all parts of the world, of high buildings and industrial plants, of the theatre and of Buffalo Bill's Wild West Show, of Harvard College at Cambridge, of the hospitals, and of the strange people he had seen, some of them black and some of them yellow. His old friends listened in rapt attention.

Grandfather saved his best story for the end: his visit to a distillery. He told them how whiskey was made by the cask. He described the vast warehouses where the whiskey was stored in bond for aging with thousands upon thousand of casks, stacked in rows from floor to ceiling, each row a hundred yards or more long. Then he tried to describe the artificial refrigeration in the distillery, with pipes covered with hoarfrost running along the walls, and tanks in the floor from which workers extricated blocks of ice, weighing hundreds of pounds.

This was too much. There were gasps from several of his auditors.

"This was in July!" exclaimed Big Malcolm Stephen, incredulously.

"That's right," replied Grandfather.

"Well, I always thought you were a damn liar, Michael Eoin," he shouted. "Now I know it."

With that Malcolm violently put his hat on his head, strode out the door, slamming it after him. He and Grandfather never spoke again, although each lived for many years afterwards and were close neighbors.

Despite this display of incredulity the average Washabuckter was credulous. Generally he believed what he heard and what he read. He expected others to tell him the truth, although he did expect a certain amount of exaggeration or belittlement. He felt that people who know enough to write newspapers, magazines and books certainly should know what they were writing about. This was true even of Grandfather, who was a prodigious reader; and Father took advantage of his credulity once to solve a family problem.

The Old Man liked what he called "store crackers." As a result there had to be an inexhaustible supply of them in the house. This was not always easy, for the nearest store was some distance from the farm and bad weather might make it impossible to get to it for weeks at a time. Every once in a while the supply would give out and Grandfather would go into a rage that would have made King Lear look like Caspar Milquetoast, and the rage would continue until the supply had been replenished. These rages finally became a family nuisance.

So Father decided to do something about them. He had recently returned from a long visit in the United States. Talking to Grandmother in the kitchen one day, but making certain that Grandfather could hear every word, he told her of having visited one of the factories where these "store crackers" were made. He painted a startling picture of huge vats filled with soft, white, watery dough being mixed by troops of big, burly, naked gorillas. Dozens of them waded about in the dough. Others stood on the rim of the vats and dove in and swam about. Occasionally they would have a game called "dough-ball" that resembled water-polo, in which they would make up teams and splash and swim about with a ball to their heart's content. It was fine sport, Father concluded.

Grandfather never said a word; but he never ate another "store cracker."

Not all Washabuckters were overawed by the big cities. The story was told there of the experience of one of the sons of Dan the Banker in New York. His ship happened to put into the port and he called upon a son of Red Rory the Piper, who had a job on the waterfront. After some talk about things back home, they set out together to see the sights. The son of Dan the Banker explained later that the son of Red Rory the Piper was determined to impress him with his superior acquaintance with the big city and its culture.

It seems they were strolling up Fifth Avenue from Madison Square. When they reached the old Waldorf-

Astoria the son of Red Rory feigned long familiarity with that famous hostelry. He strode into its sumptuous reception rooms, and finally led the son of Dan the Banker up to the desk. Thereupon the son of Red Rory the Piper banged the counter with his powerful fist and demanded:

"Is the mail from Washabuckt in yet?"

The response has not been reported, nor are there any data available on how long it took Oscar's minions to recover their poise.

No account of the Washabuckt of those days would do it justice that did not report the glorification of physical might. Many people to their sorrow considered it their most important characteristic. Much of their folklore dealt with giants. All of their heroes were strong men and they were admired solely because of their bodily prowess. Those included Sir William Wallace and Robert Bruce, who had licked the English on many battlefields; the Giant MacAskill and the Sea Wolf, who were Cape Breton boys; and John L. Sullivan, whose glorious reign had recently ended. While they liked fights and fighters and talked about them day and night they did not limit their hero worship to these. They also admired the man who could swing a powerful axe in the forest, fell an unruly horse or a roaring bull with his fist, or handle a boat in the stormy waters of the Lake. They tolerated but did not like physical weaklings.

These simple people lived a wholesome but primitive life close to the soil. Their wants were elementary and necessary and their thinking direct and concise when not confused by their inherited superstitions. They were rough and ready but kindly at heart. They looked for no favors. They would prefer to give rather than to receive. They were well equipped to care for themselves in the world they knew.

CHAPTER FIVE

An Economy Without Money

EVERY MAN IN WASHABUCKT was his own boss, for he got his livelihood from nature and did not have to work for any other man or thank any one but God for it. True, that work was sometimes hard and the living scanty and poor, but such as it was a man was always free to do as he wished and to talk as he pleased. He could take the day off and just loaf if he so desired. He did not have to toady to any one. He could hold his head high; and did.

The Washabuckter owned his own farm free and clear. It was not worth much as farms went, but it was his; there was no such thing as a mortgage. Taxes were low. A family might be in debt to one of the general stores, but the debt was seldom onerous, and could be paid with the new crop. The farm was cultivated primarily not to produce income but to yield food for the home; and the family supplemented its harvest from the waters of the Lake and the runs of the forest. There never could be a shortage of food, except in case of the illness or death of the man of the house, for all three sources could not fail at the one time. In fact, so far as I know not one of them ever did fail.

Nature was generous in producing food in Washabuckt, as it is in most places, providing that man is willing to cooperate with it. The farm animals supplied milk and butter, poultry and eggs, beef and veal, pork and mutton, the field crops yielded oats and barley, potatoes and turnips, and the orchards furnished apples and plums. A few farmers also sowed and reaped wheat and buckwheat. Other popular temperate-zone crops like cabbage and beets, parsnips and carrots, peas and lettuce, were not known, or at least they were not grown. Washabuckt was too far north and the growing season was too short for others, like corn, grapes and pears. But the lake teemed with salmon and trout, eels and cod, herring and perch, lobster and oysters, clams and mussels. The forests, too, made their contribution with nuts and maple sugar. Every pasture, in fact every hillside in the open and clearing in the woods, produced a wide variety of luscious wild strawberries, raspberries, blueberries, blackberries and mushrooms. The berries could be enjoyed fresh or they could be preserved for the winter. Finally, there was good hunting and the man of the house could come back with ducks or geese, rabbits or partridge. Thus food was not only abundant, but in wide variety for those who would help themselves to it. The energetic and industrious family could serve a good table. There were those who did not; but it was their own fault.

The storing of food in the home and the barns for the family and the farm stock started early in the spring and continued until late fall. Three or four or more barrels of herring would be salted away in the spring. Large quantities of cod would be salted first and later dried in the sun. During the summer salmon, trout, cod and eels would go fresh to Washabuckt tables, and a calf or two and a lamb or two would be butchered for fresh meat. During the winter eels and smelts would be caught through the ice on the lake, and some seals would be speared. And the snaring of rabbits and the shooting of ducks and partridge would provide both sport and tasty delicacies.

From June to September the women and the children would pick bushels of berries; dozens of bottles would be preserved.

At the harvest the farmer would fill the cellar of his home with stores of potatoes and turnips, hundreds of bushels of them, and the barns would be filled with hay, oats, barley and wheat, and sometimes buckwheat.

In the fall the farmer would do his butchering, usually slaughtering a steer and a pig or two, and salting them for the rest of the year. He might also shoot a deer or two.

With his crops harvested the farmer would take a wagonload of wheat, oats and barley to the grist-mill to be ground into meal for the family and the stock. He himself would help the miller take his bags of grain into the mill, prepare them on the roasters, and serve them to the grinders. Again this was a 50-50 proposition, one-half of the meal going to the miller for his services and that of his mill, the farmer driving home with the remainder.

Before the cold weather came and the ice covered the lake, the Washabuckter would load his boat with the products of his industry and take it across the lake to the merchants in Baddeck. He might also sell a cow, a colt, some sheep, and some hides. With these he would establish credits, after paying any debts, and in return obtain provisions and materials that he himself could not produce. He would probably buy several pounds of tea (he did not drink coffee), kerosene for his lamps, gallons of molasses, a barrel of sugar, and a barrel or two of salt, some pepper and other spices, and perhaps also a bolt or two of cotton cloth, shoes, and other necessaries.

Throughout the neighborhood it was generally understood that the women of the family who milked the cows and made the butter and fed the hens and raised the chickens and collected the eggs, in return had the privilege of marketing these products for their own benefit. With their credits they would buy notions, clothes and underwear and various little luxuries.

With the first heavy fall of snow the Washabuckt men would head for the forests to get the winter's wood, and later to do some lumbering. This they would do with a relish, for there is no more enthralling experience than the primeval forest with its first, fresh blanket of white snow, broken only by the tracks of the animals and the birds of the wilds. Great trees would be felled with a thundering crash, and cut into logs, and drawn out by sleds. After a week or two there would be a huge woodpile by each house, usually right in front of the front door, for the woodpile was a matter of family pride, like the French farm's manure heap. This wood would later be cut and split at leisure into lengths and sizes for the kitchen stoves and the fireplaces. The chips were used as kindlings.

With food, shelter and warmth provided for his family and for his stock, the Washabuckter took things easy in the long winter months. His major chore was to feed and water the stock and clean the stables, which took not more than an hour twice a day. The rest of the time he devoted to gossip with his neighbors, an occasional game of cards, frolics, a few drinking bouts and some fighting. He also found time to read the weekly newspapers; to study the reports from the provincial experimental farm at Truro; and to contemplate the affairs of the community, the province of Nova Scotia, the Dominion of Canada, and the world in general. He had little to worry about, for at its worst life was not unkind. He was not wealthy but he certainly had an abundance of everything he needed and plenty of time to enjoy it.

It was different with the women. In Washabuckt as

elsewhere their work never ended, summer or winter. The work of the home was theirs at all times, and no man would bestir himself to interfere or help with the cooking, the cleaning or the washing. If there were children they would, of course, help in the home as they did on the farm, bringing in the wood, carrying the water in buckets from the well, and washing the dishes. All were taught to make themselves useful.

There were no gadgets or machines to do the farm or house work or to make it easier; and no one ever thought for an instant that such things were necessary. Work was something to be done; and the father of the family would occasionally refer to the Biblical injunction that man must earn his bread by the sweat of his brow, but more often to the Gaelic proverb to the effect that it is the idle hand that throws the cat into the fire.

Despite the multifarious duties of the home and the farm, the women found time to spin and knit and weave and make clothes for the family and also to hook rag rugs for the floors, some of the latter of beautiful designs and colorings. Most of this work was done sitting about the fire during the winter nights.

Every farm had a flock of sheep. The crop of wool was washed and carded and spun into yarn. The old women did all of the carding and spinning, singing or humming Gaelic songs to the rhythm of the carding brushes or of the spinning wheels as they did so, but not without watching every activity of the home and hearing every morsel of gossip. With the wool finally converted into large balls of white, gray and black yarn, and perhaps some of it dyed into other colors, all the women and girls of the family got busy with their knitting needles and soon it was made into socks, stockings, mitts and sweaters. Some of these would be sold or traded to get feminine finery.

Most families also had a loom, usually in the attic,

and some of the yarn would be woven into yards and yards of homespun cloth. This also was the work of the old ladies. When large bolts were available the family would have a "milling frolic" to "mill," or soften, the heavy, warm but coarse cloth and give it a nap. A long bench would be set up in the kitchen. A capable singer with a repertory of Gaelic songs would sit at the head of the bench, with six or seven young ladies along each side. The leader would start a long lilting song and as she did so the "milling" would begin, the girls along the sides joining lustily in the chorus, and all beating and thumping the cloth against the bench in time to the tune. Later the young men would appear with a fiddler and perhaps a bagpiper, refreshments would be served, and all would eat and dance until morning. Later the "milled" homespun would be made into coats, pants, skirts, underwear and blankets.

The men of the family did the cobbling. In the early days the pioneers made their own shoes and boots, including the tanning of the hides. Later they only did the repairing and the resoling and this from purchased leather, for they found it easier and cheaper to sell their hides and buy what leather they needed. The men also did their own barbering. Some of them were quite adept at such things, but, adept or not, there was no choice in the matter, for there were no professional cobblers or barbers in the community; and anyway no one would think of spending money for such services.

Neither was there any dry-cleaning or pressing of garments. Nothing was worn that could not be washed and ironed and thus kept clean and presentable. Anyway, clothes were worn for warmth and to cover nakedness and not for pride and exhibitionism. The clothes did not make the Washabuckt man or woman, who did not resort to such artifices to impress their neighbors, for they knew that it was the body that the clothes covered and the mind that mattered. They were simple and innocent in many things, but not in this.

Living mostly in the open air, with plenty of simple food, lots of invigorating work, and almost no worry, the people of Washabuckt were rarely sick. The nearest physician was in Baddeck and generally this meant a four- or five-mile trip across the Lake by boat over the water or by sleigh over the ice to get him, as he could not be called by telephone. Sometimes, as when the ice was forming or breaking, no physician could be obtained. Usually when the physician was called it meant that the patient was on the point of death. The Washabuckter was not in the habit of consulting doctors for trivial illnesses, or imaginary ones, and did not always have the cash that a doctor's services would require. Dentists were unknown. Both teeth and toothaches were ignored.

The average housewife had her own medicines and could make good use of them. A hot foot-bath with plenty of mustard in the scalding water was a standard remedy for all sorts of chills or colds and the patient was then bundled off to a warm bed. For most other incipient illness a dose of epsom salts was used, and the mere threat of the remedy would cure most of the ailments of the children. In the spring every member of the family got doses of sulphur and molasses, and was encouraged thereafter to remain outdoors. The neighborhood midwife delivered all the children and treated most feminine disorders; and considered the opportunity of sharing the gossip of the visiting women adequate reward for her services. Anyway, it was the only compensation she got.

Without the benefit of physicians, longevity was the rule in Washabuckt and not the exception. Men and women lived into their eighties, their nineties, and occasionally one passed the hundred mark. The person that died in the early seventies was considered to have passed on in comparative youth. Moreover, the old people retained all their faculties almost to the end and kept busy with the duties of the farm and the home. Most deaths came finally from the disintegration of extreme old age, and any one dying from any other cause would be the subject of gossip for a decade or longer. There was only one violent death, a murder, in the history of the countryside, so far as I know.

MY BROTHER MURDOCH AND I gave this economy without money a good trial and proved its worth, inexperienced though we were. When he was thirteen and I seventeen years old, father placed us in a furnished house on a farm he owned and then left us to carry on his work in New England. Before departing he put in a supply of food staples, provided us with necessary clothes, and opened an account for us at the local store. For the rest he left us definitely on our own.

We had to do our own housekeeping, including all the cleaning, washing and ironing, and the cooking and baking, there being no laundries, bakeries or delicatessens. We had two cows to supply milk and butter, a dozen or so hens to furnish eggs and chickens, and each of us had a horse to ride. We had to feed and care for this farm stock, to plant some potatoes, turnips and other vegetables for our own table, and to cut and make enough hay for the two cows and the two horses, and perhaps some for sale. We also had to cut our own wood in the forest for heating and cooking.

Two boys never had more fun. We made quick work of the household and farm chores and thus had plenty of time for riding the countryside on our horses; for shooting game, snaring rabbits, trapping fur-bearing animals; and for fishing in the Lake or the streams. Every week or so we would set a net and catch a haul of fish or we would spear eels or catch lobsters. At all times we had an abundance of fresh game and fish, which we would cook for ourselves, give to the neighbors, or place to our credit at the store. Every day that the weather allowed we were outdoors; and when it did not we stayed at home and cooked and cleaned. We spent the evenings reading, unless there was a frolic or a shindig within riding distance.

Soon after Father's departure we got the notion that the farm needed a new barn, and we decided it would be a good idea to surprise him by building one.

We started work on the barn by heading into the forest with our axes. During the winter we cut down enough timber to build two barns and hauled the logs to the sawmill. When it had been sawed we trucked our half home. Then a neighborhood expert offered to help us put up the frame. A couple of other neighbors also volunteered to help us get going. So we made a party of it. The frame was erected during one day, and every one ate and made merry far into the night. We ourselves carried on from there, and in about three more months the barn was ready for its tenants. All we bought for its construction were several kegs of nails, hinges for the doors and glass for the windows.

The barn was forty feet by eighteen feet with a fourteen-foot post and a peak roof. It was designed on the lines of the neighborhood barns, with stables for horses and cows, a shelter for the sheep, and a pigpen. It had big haymows and bins for grain. It was a large undertaking for two boys; but again it was fun.

We were on our own for fifteen months until Father sent Murdoch back to school and me to college at Antigonish. The experience had made us sturdy, self-reliant boys, and it was doubtless time well spent for both of us. When Father came to settle with the local merchant he found that our debit for the fifteen months was twenty-two dollars and some odd cents. This compared favorably with the record made by Henry David Thoreau at

Walden Pond, for while he only built a shack we built a large barn, and we served a varied table while he lived mostly on beans. Moreover, we did not hire out to any one for wages or for any purpose; on the contrary we were able to help out our neighbors with work or food on many occasions and to offer hospitality to our many friends at all times.

This hospitality of ours recalls an incident that is worth passing on. In the fall of the year the forests were full of hazel and beech nuts. Murdoch liked the hazel nuts, but neither of us cared much for the beech nuts. Murdoch, with my help, gathered large quantities of hazel nuts. They were, of course, in their husks and Murdoch spent the nights of a week removing the husks. This done, he had a bushel basket full of nuts, and looked forward to the pleasure of eating them all winter.

Soon thereafter we were honored by a visit from Big Mary, the neighborhood schoolteacher, and Little Bess, her sister. Each was immense, at least six feet tall and a couple of yards about the beam. It took a bolt of cloth to make one of them a dress and when they moved ponderously along the Washabuckt roads in the autumnal winds they looked like two full-rigged barques out of Halifax. Their appetites were in keeping with their dimensions.

Their visit took us by surprise and strained our hospitality. Finally Murdoch thought of the nuts. Kind of heart and also eager to impress the two Amazons he produced the bushel basket, instead of merely serving a few nuts in a bowl. He placed it on the floor between them and gave each a nutcracker. They went to work on the nuts, dropping the shells on the floor. Murdoch and I sat back to enjoy the spectacle. Our enjoyment was not long-lived, for we soon realized to our amazement that they had somehow got the idea that we intended them to eat all the nuts, the whole basketful, and they did not intend to disappoint us.

Murdoch and I decided that if we were going to have any nuts for ourselves we had better do so before the two ladies had disposed of them. As there were no more nut-crackers we got hammers and went to work. The nuts did not last long, only an hour or so.

The two ladies left none the worse for their unusual feast and without anything but the usual perfunctory word of thanks. It took Murdoch two weeks to get over his loss. He felt much as would a squirrel whose winter store had been robbed by some forest marauder.

THEN THERE WAS THE TIME that Copper Jack cooked the loon, also known as the great northern diver. We liked Copper Jack; we enjoyed his stories. He had traveled over the United States and Canada and Alaska, doing all sorts of jobs, and he had been in and out of the best jails in both countries. He had been tagged Copper Jack after an affair of some sort with copper scrap, an early adventure.

Copper Jack's tales never suffered in the telling and he was always the hero of them, or at least he came out on top in every exploit. He bragged much about his cooking and, until proved a liar in this as in many other things, had insisted that he had been the chief cook at the Waldorf-Astoria in New York, and had in fact prepared the food for a famous banquet for President McKinley. We had him to dinner on evening and served wild duck, and it was good and tasty, but Copper Jack spent the evening telling us how to cook duck, and what he could do to duck, and how he once won compliments from "Diamond Jim" Brady, who, he claimed, was a friend of his, or at least one of the admirers of his prowess as a cook.

About a week later a lonely loon from the far north sat down on a pond on our property, right by the Lake but having no outlet into it. It came in a storm, for it could only lift its heavy body into a strong wind and it was trapped there when the weather turned calm. Murdoch and I discovered it and decided to have some royal sport. First of all, a loon seldom came that far south, and again it is one of the most difficult of birds to shoot, for it is forever on the alert, and was supposed to dive at the flash of the gun and before the bullet could reach it.

Murdoch posted himself on one side of the pond and I hid on the other. We had a 30-30 Winchester rifle which Father had used in the Klondike and a double-barreled shotgun. As the loon swam about the pond we took turns in firing at it; but we could not score a hit. It would dive and a split second later the bullets would splash in the water where it had just disappeared.

So we decided to trick it. We fired one shot into the air, got it to dive, and watched for it to surface. Then we shot with both guns before it had got set to dive again. After several attempts we got it.

We took the loon home with us; and then arose the question what to do with it. Murdoch thought it would be a good idea to mount it and keep it as a family trophy. The trouble with that was that there probably was not a taxidermist nearer than Boston. Then we got a really brilliant idea. It came almost simultaneously to both of us. Why not dress it, pretend it was a wild goose, and get Copper Jack to cook it? The point to this is that a loon is inedible, for it is as tough as rubber and of about the same consistency.

Copper Jack not only consented to cook the "goose," but at his suggestion we made the affair a "banquet." We invited Grandfather, the local merchant and others among the local gentry and local wits, a total of eleven in all, and, including Murdoch, Copper Jack and myself, we made a total of fourteen.

Early on the appointed day Copper Jack arrived with an extra-large pan, some purchases from the local store, and some "exotic" herbs unknown to Washabuckt cuisine, but which, Murdoch and I suspected, probably correctly, had begun life as weeds in one of the neighboring pastures. He dressed and stuffed the "goose" and made an apple pie. Murdoch and I had made some bread and cake the day before. We had a sprightly fire in the kitchen stove.

As the "goose" was sizzling gaily and beginning to brown the guests started to arrive. They all sat in the kitchen, as was the Washabuckt custom, to marvel at Copper Jack's performance. The aroma from the cooking "goose" permeated the kitchen and the house and ultimately a large part of the countryside, and was both a delight and an invitation. Copper Jack was in his element, and put on a grand show.

A small, quick-moving man, nervous and voluble, he pranced about the stove, opening the oven every few minutes to baste the bird, each time letting out a new flood of appetizing odors. Meanwhile he kept up a line of conversation, partly self-adulation and partly to stir the imagination of the dinner guests. "Ain't she a beaut, Gents?" he would remark as he opened the oven, and gave the audience a glance at the "goose." "Cooking is the greatest of the arts, Gents," he would brag, strutting about with a large spoon in his fist. "President McKinley would love this, Gents. Think how lucky you are." "Only Copper Jack could do it this way, Gents." "I'm wasting time in Washabuckt, Gents. Only Paris could appreciate my cooking." "Look at that rich brown crust, Gents. Ain't that something!" There seemed to be no end to his prattle, as he played upon the appetite of his admirers. All mouths present were watering. Murdoch and I began to have misgivings; for it began to look as if Copper Jack would make something out of that loon after all.

Finally Copper Jack pronounced the "goose" cooked to his satisfaction. Certainly it was something to behold. Brown and crisp, with stuffing and grease oozing from it, and exuding a flood of redolent cooking perfumes, it was placed on a platter and set at the head of the table. The guests sat around. Grandfather was invited to do the carving, to which he agreed with a show of reluctance, insisting for some minutes that Copper Jack should have the honor of carving his own masterpiece and apportioning it to the honored guests.

At last Grandfather tried to cut into the bird. The knife went no further than crisp crust. He stopped and tried the edge of the knife with his finger. The knife seemed sharp enough. He tried the bird again. After several attempts he stopped and asked for a scythe stone and put a new edge on the weapon. Then he tackled the "goose" once again, and this time by exerting all his great strength he did hack off some hunks and limbs, which were passed around the table.

The "banquet" guests tried to eat the "goose," but no one could disguise that it was tough, so tough, in fact, that it could not be eaten despite the raging appetites and the powerful jaws about that table. There were some remarks about his cooking that were not complimentary to Copper Jack, who for once in his life was dumbfounded into silence. The guests ate their fill of the bread, the vegetables, and the pie and the cake, and left.

A few days later Copper Jack announced that he was going back "to the States." And go he did. He was never seen in Washabuckt again.

Our hospitality was in keeping with the hospitality of Washabuckt. These Scots were never so poor that they would not share whatever they had, much or little, good or bad, with their neighbors or anybody in need. No one had ever been known to refuse food or lodging.

Knowing this Scottish trait, it has pained me to hear of the Scots being "tight," and to have to listen eternally to inane and stupid jokes, especially in New York, about it. This reputation doubtless had its origin in the Lowlanders of Scotland, whom the Celtic Scots, of the Highlands and Islands, consider English. In the Barra Gaelic, spoken in Washabuckt, one word indicated both Lowlander and Englishman, and there was no way to distinguish between one and the other, nor did these Scots think it necessary to do so.

Every one was welcome in a Washabuckt home. The visitor walked right in without knocking, knowing that he would be greeted cheerfully and that the host and his family would have nothing to conceal. On entering he took a seat without being invited to do so. The women of the house would start brewing tea, and he would be served this and whatever else the home afforded. If the visitor stayed for the night, or for a week or more, he was also welcome. In fact, a frolic might be arranged to make things pleasant for him.

Nor did the visitor have to be known. Those from other neighborhoods and strangers and peddlers were equally welcome. I remember a deserter from a French warship in Sydney who came to Grandfather's home. He could not speak English and of course knew no Gaelic; but the old man guessed what he was doing and what he wanted. Grandfather indicated by signs that he would get food and lodging; and then proceeded to do what he could to make the worried Frenchman comfortable and his visit agreeable. Everything else failing, the old man sang Gaelic songs for the deserter until it was time to retire, and then led him to his bed and tucked him in for the night. After a hearty breakfast next morning, the visitor tried to hand fifty cents first to Grandmother and then to me as a token of his gratitude, but Grandfather handed him back the coin and sent him on his way with his blessing. We never heard of him again.

Another French deserter in a nearby neighborhood was not so fortunate. He arrived at a home where modern ideas had diluted the old forms of hospitality. This family pretended to make him welcome, and then sent a boy to the authorities to inform on him, hoping for a reward. The deserter was arrested and taken back to his ship and bondage, perhaps in Devil's Island. Some time later this family boiled the family dinner in a pot that had been used to mix Paris green to kill potato bugs, and all members of it were dead within the hour. You cannot tell their neighbors, and certainly not the Washabuckters, that this was not retribution for their violation of the Scottish code.

At least once a year, and sometimes twice, Grandfather entertained Micmac Indians from the reservation near Middle River, across the lake. These Indians were usually led by Little Bill, a venerable and ageless but seedy and disreputable patriarch, who claimed to be more than one hundred years old and looked it. Little Bill was always accompanied by his favorite daughter, who had had eight children by eight different fathers, all without benefit of clergy, and at that time had excellent prospects of eight more. They came to Washabuckt to sell baskets, all well made and of beautiful primitive designs, and other handicrafts. Grandfather was a favorite customer, for he not only bought their products, but fed them the best in the house and invited them to stay for the night. They always stayed; in fact they counted on his invitation.

Grandfather enjoyed these visits and would hold long and earnest conversations with Little Bill, or his understudy, in which much earthy wisdom would be exchanged; but the women of the house did not enjoy them, for Little Bill and his companions were dirty and smelly, and carriers of fleas, bedbugs, lice and all other species of vermin that could survive in that climate on a diet of Indian. Over and over again Grandmother and my aunts would protest and rage, but it was of no use, for the old gentleman had his code of hospitality, and the Indians would be welcome on their next visit.

"I have never turned a hungry man from my door," he would say with emphasis, "and I am not going to do so now."

After each visit the women would spend days scrubbing and scouring and washing before they felt the house was clean again.

The ultimate in Scottish hospitality, according to Grandfather, was reached by a poor widow on Boularderie, a large island in the Bras d'Or Lakes, and he himself was the recipient of it. In his younger days he worked for a time at Cow Bay. As he was returning to Washabuckt afoot he was overtaken with fatigue and hunger, so he dropped into a home beside the road for food and rest. It turned out to be the home of the widow and her five young children.

The lady was visibly embarrassed by his visit but she insisted on his staying. When she left the room he was appalled by the evidences of poverty. Soon he heard wild and agonizing shrieks from a pig in the barnyard. Grandfather thought little of it at first, but when the shrieks continued he began to wonder.

Some twenty minutes later the widow invited Grandfather to sit at the table. There he was astounded to discover that she had cut the ears and tail off the living pig and served them to him for his dinner. As Grandfather ate, the pig continued to shriek.

Needless to say, Grandfather did not enjoy the dinner any more than did the unfortunate pig; but for the rest of his life he extolled the widow's spirit of hospitality.

The charity of the people of Washabuckt was as simple and kindly as was their hospitality. It consisted in taking care of their own. It had a community spirit that is rare these days, anywhere. Their old folks, no matter how senile and decrepit, even if bedridden for years, were kept in their homes and made to feel welcome. Moreover, they were treated with respect. The same was true of the mentally deficient and the deformed. They were never permitted to feel burdensome; and in fact they seldom were, for they could be helpful about the farms and the homes. Widows and orphans were helped to live on in their own homes on their own farms.

There were, of course, public institutions to take care of such persons; but they got no tenants from Washabuckt. The idea never occurred to these Scots, although they knew about the institutions. Nor did they like persons who did not take care of their own. There was the case of a wealthy merchant in Baddeck, who sent an aged relative to the poorhouse. Many of his customers deserted him at once, for they felt that he was not a fit person with whom to do business. They never trusted him again.

The Washabuckt people enjoyed their charities, for they made them pleasant occasions such as another excuse for a frolic. Take for instance a planting frolic. The boys and girls of the neighborhood would gather on the farm of some widow or aged couple and would spend the long day planting the crops. If seeds, horses and implements were needed, these would be provided. Towards evening the girls would prepare a feast from baskets they had brought with them. After all had eaten well, fiddlers or pipers would appear and all would dance far into the night. Sometimes the affair might end in a good fight as some of the men would be certain to do some drinking and all loved fighting.

There would be more frolics for the fencing, the harvesting, the plowing, and the cutting of the winter's wood. These frolics took the place of the movies as sources of entertainment. The recipients of the charity always joined in the fun and there was never any condescension or humiliation about it.

At this time in Washabuckt there was a lady in her late middle age, let us say, who had no home or farm of her own and no immediate relatives to support her. So she lived on the neighborhood. She would stay in home after home, a week or two in each, until she had made the round of the community. She was known as Big Sarah and was not only a Washabuckt character but a general favorite. She was welcome everywhere, for she was a capable gossip-gatherer and could tell a good story. She was the predecessor and patron saint of the modern gossip-columnist and served the same purpose.

Big Sarah carried herself with stately dignity, which was not easy for her, as some girlhood injury to her ankles had twisted her feet outward. She had at least twenty versions of how this happened. She was always neatly dressed and clean, could sew and knit expertly, and was the spirit of romance. At times she would help with the housework, the washing or the haymaking; but she scorned working for pay. She was content to be received as an honored guest or at least as a member of the family and to share the benefits and the responsibilities that the latter involved. She never complained, although there were reports that her tongue could be bitter and sharp.

Old Sarah, as she was sometimes known, had never had any formal education and could not read or write. She insisted, however, that she could do both, and liked to tell young listeners about her school days—days of romance as well as study. She would pick up a book or a newspaper and spend hours at a time in "reading." And she would tell of her correspondence, although no one ever saw a letter, with the young bloods of her day, now residing in the Boston States.

Once when she was holding the newspaper upside down and feigning reading, a young wag pressed her for the news of the day. She tried to ignore him; but on his continued insistence she told him of murders and other crimes, and concluded:

"There has been a terrible storm on the Grand Banks

and a big ship turned upside down. All the crew was drowned."

There was a picture of a schooner in the newspaper.

OLD BLACK HECTOR unwittingly expressed Washabuckt philosophy on his death bed.

In his day Black Hector was a dashing young man with subtle humor and a roguish delight in flaunting the local social conventions. He married a charming and beautiful French lady from Arichat and proceeded to beget nine children. With a household full of bawling brats he left her and the community and from then on showed no more interest in his offspring than did Jean Jacques Rousseau, another lover of nature and the natural life, although unknown to Hector.

When he was an old man and obviously dying, his French wife in her charity rushed to his bedside to nurse him and to prepare him for the end. She forgave him his trespasses, which were not few, and when she had him ready to meet his God, Whom she hoped would be equally forgiving, she asked him:

"What are you going to leave me, Hector?"

With the old roguish glint in his black eyes, he looked at her for a moment and replied:

"Ain't I leaving you the whole world! What more could you want?"

CHAPTER SIX

The Ghosts Cross the Atlantic

WHEN THE MACNEILS and the MacLeans sailed the Ocean from Barra to Nova Scotia, their ghosts came along with them and made themselves right at home in Washabuckt. These spirits seemed to have enjoyed the long journey and to have thrived in their new surroundings, for in my days in Washabuckt they were both vigorous and active. Moreover, they were numerous, picturesque and adequate for all occasions.

There were all kinds of spirits about Washabuckt, spirits that haunted houses and beset families, and spirits that roamed the countryside, especially at night. The people of Washabuckt believed that departed souls in trouble returned to their old fields and homes and remained there until their kinsmen had expiated their sins by making amends for some wrong they had done in life. They believed that Satan and his imps prowled about Washabuckt from sunset until dawn tempting people to do wrong; and they were ready, indeed anxious, to blame these evil spirits for their own evil doings, especially when they were drunk or unusually belligerent. Like the Irish, they also believed in Fairies, although the little people were not as influential in Washabuckt as I later found them to be in Ireland. Good spirits were also about, it seems, but one heard so little about them that I got the impression that they were distinctly in the minority.

Washabuckters had implicit faith in a variety of superstitions, and these guided many of their activities. The validity of none of them was ever questioned, and these good people were ready at all times to accept new ones, no matter where they came from. They also put great store in all kinds of omens and auguries; and some of these were always being seen before tragic events, like a sudden death in a family. Then, of course, they believed in the evil eye and second sight.

The belief in such things is easier to understand than to explain. As I have mentioned, they were not questioned, but if they had been the average adult could have related many experiences of his own with ghosts and omens and the evil eye; and that would end it. These things were true to him because he had seen or heard them. You could not convince him that his eyesight or hearing could be at fault; and certainly you could not convince him that his imagination had gone on a rampage.

In fact, one of the favorite pastimes on a cold winter's night in Washabuckt was to gather about the fireplace and tell ghost stories in the dim light of the kerosene lamp. These harrowing tales could freeze the marrow of your bones, for they were told with conviction and in graphic detail, and they always dealt with places and persons familiar to the listeners. With the northern winds howling outside in the dark night and sometimes making the house itself shudder, the atmosphere was ideal, and even a skeptic would enter into the mood of the occasion, so that he would find himself believing what he knew he could not believe. So stirring were some of these seances that guests would linger long after they should go, for they did not want to walk out into the night, and the children would be afraid to go to bed.

Of course some storytellers were better than others. Some were so expert in fact at picturing the eerie and occult and had so varied and extensive a repertory that they were in constant demand like popular after-dinner speakers in New York. There is much art in the proper telling of a ghost story, an art that was cultivated assiduously in Washabuckt. The story had to have the right mixture of suspense and horror and reach its climax with ease and grace. The details had to conform to local conceptions. Then there was a definite tone of voice that was most effective; and the voice had to be modulated from an insinuating whisper to a blood-curdling roar. The real experts knew well how to play upon the imagination of their audiences, for they had as much understanding of the human love of horror as had any police reporter of a metropolitan newspaper.

Ghosts always have their favorite playgrounds and the most popular of all in the Catholic Washabuckt was the Protestant graveyard. This was on a point of land that jutted into the lake about a mile and a half from Grandfather's farm. In its quiet, rustic bosom rested the dead of the three Protestant families in the community. There were about twenty graves in all under the beautiful trees, each with a modest headstone. The place had an atmosphere of repose and dignity, and yet it seems it bred more ghosts than the New Jersey meadows do mosquitoes.

This amazed me, for these families, whose ancestors came from the Island of Lewis, near Barra in the Hebrides, were highly respected and well treated by their neighbors in life, although the natives of Barra considered them aliens and strangers and resented their Lewis accent—a soft, lingering drawl something like Alabama English. As a boy I had looked forward hopefully to a Lewis funeral with its foreign rites and the inevitable ghost, or shoal of ghosts to follow; but none of these kindly and otherwise considerate people obliged me by dying while I was a resident of the community, so I did not have a chance to study things firsthand. Instead they went on living happily and contentedly, long-lived like other Washabuckt people, and unconscious of my morbid expectations.

Of the fact that the Protestant cemetery swarmed with ghosts, however, there could be no doubt in Washabuckt, for the evidence was overwhelming. Almost every one who passed the area at night heard unearthly howls and saw queer specters in the bushes near the road. But I never knew of these ghosts ever doing any one any harm, aside from congealing the blood and terrorizing the souls of passers-by. The immediate neighborhood was not considered safe even in broad daylight, and most people, and especially women and children, would walk the road with uneasy step until they were past the graveyard and then would move quickly about their business.

On a dare my brother and I entered the graveyard one bright day, not because we had the courage to enter but because we lacked the courage not to do so. We expected all kinds of dire happenings; but nothing did happen. All we heard was the gentle ripple of the waters of the Lake on the shore and the rustle of the leaves of some poplar trees. We stepped gingerly among the graves and read some of the inscriptions on the tombstones and picked a handful of daisies that were unconscious of their heroism. From then on my brother and I commanded the respect of all the boys and girls in our school; and made much of it.

There was only one skeptic in Washabuckt; and that was my Father. He did not fear ghosts for he did not believe in them; and as I pictured him in those days he feared neither man nor devil. He did not spend much time in Washabuckt, but when he was there he loved to ridicule the ghost stories and to poke fun at all the local superstitions. Big Sarah remarked one day that he had nothing to fear, for the devil respected his own. When Father heard this he laughed heartily. Others predicted that the devil would get him in the end; and some of the members of his own family were none too sure that they were not right.

Father was a great visitor and he did most of his visiting alone and at night. He enjoyed walking in the moonlight or swinging a kerosene lantern in the darkness. I admired his reckless courage in thus exposing himself.

One moonlight night when the snows made the entire world white he returned to Grandfather's home early and in a hurry.

"What's the matter?" Grandmother asked him in Gaelic.

"I've seen a ghost," he replied.

"Where?"

"In the Protestant graveyard. I heard it first; then I saw it."

With that he got Grandfather's double-barreled shotgun. Then he found two shells and removed the buckshot and replaced it with rock salt.

"What are you doing?" Grandfather inquired.

"I'm going to have some fun, too," he replied, stepping out into the night.

Father returned along the road past the graveyard. Again he heard unearthly moans and yowls coming from a clump of bushes on the cemetery side of the road. He stopped short and gazed in the direction of the sounds. Then raising the gun to his shoulder he moved slowly towards the sounds. As he did so the sounds ceased abruptly and a white figure stirred the brushes. Father fired a shell at the figure, which threw aside a bed sheet and started off on the run. Father followed the figure a distance and then fired the second shell at it.

The ghost turned out to be a neighbor, who must for our purposes remain anonymous, but who, as Father afterwards related, "spent a fortnight picking the salt out of his tail."

On another night, this one dark, two terror-stricken neighbors arrived at Grandfather's house in a condition of near collapse. When they could do so they explained that they had encountered a ghost on the road past our farm, "right in the middle of the road" and blocking all passage. It was a huge dark mass, they said, that moved in all directions, meanwhile emitting queer grunts and moans. It seemed to have no head or tail and to be neither man nor beast. When it moved in their direction that finished them; they ran for the first refuge, which was Grandfather's home.

Father asked them to return with him and show it to him. No amount of pleading could get them to do so and they prayed Father to have nothing to do with it. Father took a lantern and set out alone to locate it. He was not long in doing so, and in the light of the lantern it turned out to be a pig in a bag.

Donald the Piper had bought this pig from a neighbor, put it in the bag, and thrown it onto his cart to take home. Then Donald and the neighbor celebrated the transaction with some drinks so that when the joggling cart dumped the pig on the road Donald did not miss it and continued gaily on his way. The pig in the bag on the road in the dark was indeed a strange thing to meet, for the poor pig could not control its movements and like Stephen Leacock's horseman went off in all directions, meanwhile bemoaning its fate. Father rescued the pig and a sober Donald got it the next day.

Next in popularity to the Protestant cemetery as a happy hunting ground for ghosts was the "murder farm," the scene of a murder some twenty-five years before my time, and the only murder in the history of Washabuckt.

There had been a frolic in the "murder house," which ended in a battle royal, and one man, a weakling, drew a knife and stabbed one of the best-liked young men of the community. The victim bled to death, and the slayer served time in the penitentiary. The foul crime doomed the home. The family moved out and left the neighborhood; the farm was abandoned; and the ghosts moved in. When I knew it all that was left on the site were the foundations of the house and barn, and these were a mass of thistles, nettles and burdocks. Except for a nest of snakes, no living creature lived in or near what had been a happy home.

People did not like to talk about the "murder farm." They would not trespass upon its fields or wood lot, although these might well have been public property. It was understood that no one wanted the land so until I left there had been no effort to sell it for taxes. The neighbors did not even want their cattle to graze in its open and fenceless fields, for they believed that the grass would sour the milk, and certainly it would not bring any one any luck. It was a sort of No Man's Land.

The ghosts that dwelt on the "murder farm" were supposed to be particularly daring and vicious. There were reports about that Satan himself had been seen there, and he was said to be considering making it a resort farm, a cooling-off spot after Hell's fires. I heard many furtive references to this and other stories about the place; but when I made direct inquiries all I got were excuses for not discussing the matter further or blank silence. I gave the "murder farm" a wide berth by day and was never in the vicinity alone by night. One thing about it was obvious, and that was that crime did not pay in Washabuckt.

I do not want to give the impression that the Washabuckt ghosts and spirits were limited to a few areas or scenes, for they were all over the community, and might put in an appearance anywhere any time. Moreover, there were all species of them, and there was not a ghostly duty or function that they did not perform. Some of them were more versatile than others, and more terrifying; and none of them seemed to have any inhibitions. Sometimes they would appear as lights that would prance and gallop about and make great leaps in the air. Sometimes they would appear in human form. All of the latter seemed able to yowl and groan in the most ghastly manner, but whether any of them could speak was never known, for no one ever got to the point (or remained long enough on the scene) of trying them out, either in Gaelic or English.

During my time in Washabuckt an old kinsman and near neighbor of ours died rather suddenly. He had been a virtuous and wise man in his day and the father of a large family. After a proper wake and funeral it was discovered that he had left a will bequeathing all his property to his youngest son, one of six. He also had five daughters. The other ten children got nothing. The youngest son and his family took over the homestead, and the other sons and daughters went their way, grumbling.

The youngest son had fantastic ideas for Washabuckt, ideas beyond his purse and his intelligence. He started to make over the home and the farm and to dissipate the old man's carefully gathered substance with scandalous relish. Old friends and relatives, including Grandfather, spoke to him; but he paid no heed to them.

Then one day a passer-by reported seeing the old man repairing the neglected fences of the farm—in broad daylight, so that there could be no doubt of it. A hired girl a few days later went down to the brook to do the washing, and looking up from her work she saw the old man standing silent on a rock before her. She quit on the spot. From then on there was scarcely a day or a night that he did not put in an appearance somewhere about the farm.

I remember Grandfather and Grandmother discussing the affair and wondering what was troubling the old man's soul and what should be done about it. Finally Grandfather drove to Iona to see the parish priest and had some masses said for the repose of the troubled soul. His specter was never seen again.

The best example I know of a ghost crossing the Atlantic, however, was not in Washabuckt, but about ten miles from our place and across the Lake. This Protestant family had left the Islands of Scotland and came to Cape Breton just to get away from this ghost, but he came right along with them. It seems that, a century or two before, a son of this family had killed his old and bearded father, and cut off his head. From then on whenever there was a death in that family, the beheaded father appeared on horseback, holding the reins in one hand and the bearded head in the other, and rode about the house in great circles and at a furious pace, never halting from the fall of darkness upon the earth until the crow of the cock announced the dawn.

The family naturally did not like it, but no matter what they did, good or bad, the old boy returned for every wake. Finally in desperation they moved to the New World. All went well until there was a death, and then the old beheaded ghost started his wild riding anew. Grandfather said he knew people who had seen this ghost; and so terrifying was the sight that they never were the same again. This family's wakes were not popular with their neighbors, and Grandfather had never attended one, but he believed the story.

Personally I never saw a ghost in Washabuckt or anywhere else and never hope to see one, so I have no evidence of my own to offer, and can only report what I had heard others tell. However, I did have a personal experience with the evil eye, and to this I can testify, simply telling what I saw and heard.

Grandfather and I were riding in our buggy one day. We stopped to pass the time of day with a neighbor. Grandfather and the neighbor asked about each other's families and about their crops, and made small talk about other matters. In the course of the conversation I noticed the neighbor looking intently at Old Maud, Grandfather's mare, which was standing relaxed and glad of the chance to rest.

"That's a fine animal you have, Michael Eoin," remarked the neighbor.

"Indeed and she is, and may Saint Columba bless her," replied Grandfather.

Shortly after this we were again on our way; but something had happened to Old Maud. The mare limped badly in her hind right foot, so badly in fact that she could make progress only with difficulty. I was doing the driving. I thought she might have picked up a stone in her shoe, or that a nail or stone had injured her hoof. I got out and examined the hoof and found nothing was wrong with it. We drove on and Old Maud was as lame as ever.

Grandfather, who was watching this performance in silence, finally spoke.

"That neighbor has the evil eye," he said. "That is why I asked for St. Columba's blessing on the poor creature. I was trying to save her. Water off silver will cure the spell. So let her move along gently until we reach some water."

This we did. When we reached a small brook I stopped the horse and Grandfather lent me a silver coin. Under his instructions I held it in my cupped hand and dipped some water from the stream. I rubbed the water first and then the coin on Old Maud's leg and hoof.

After some of this Grandfather remarked:

"That will do."

I got back in the buggy and we drove off. Old Maud's limp was gone; in fact I never saw her more happy or more sprightly.

I never encountered a case of second sight but I heard of many instances of it. One that I heard Grandmother tell I shall relate, for it dealt with a member of our own family. Grandfather was present when she told the story, and it must be correct in every detail for he did not contradict or interrupt her.

One evening a stranger came to Grandfather's home while their children were young. He was invited to stay for the night; and did. During the evening, both Grandmother and Grandfather noticed him looking at one of their young daughters and then looking in a corner of the room. They thought little about it; and in the morning the stranger left.

Some weeks later Grandfather received a letter from the stranger, a letter of thanks and also of embarrassment. He regretted, he wrote, to report that he had seen this young daughter laid out in a coffin in a corner of the room, and after much thought, had decided that he should tell Grandfather about it, even if it did shock him. Actually this young daughter, who had been in most vigorous health at the time of the visitor's stay had already died and had been buried before Grandfather received the letter. She had been laid out in the kind of coffin he described in the letter, and the bier had stood in the corner of the room at which he had gazed.

THE PEOPLE OF WASHABUCKT also paid great attention to the phases of the moon and guided many of their activities by them. They knew that the moon affected the tides in the Lake, and they went beyond that to believe that it affected life in its waters. They were convinced, for instance, that the flesh of the lobster and of shellfish was only full at the full of the moon, and some went so far as to believe that it was fit to eat only at such times. They also believed that the moon influenced the sap in the trees. They would cut some trees only in certain quarters of the moon at definite periods of the year. They felt that some quarters were best for the planting of the crops and some for the harvesting. They had, of course, all the popular superstitions about the moon, and some of their own. The women were always eager to have a man point out the new moon to them, for they were certain it brought them good luck.

These Scots had an elaborate and extensive folklore, including tales mixing up fairies, giants, mythical heroes, serpents, dragons, mermaids and what not. All these tales were in Gaelic and had been passed down from one generation to another from the beginning of time. None of them has ever been recorded so far as I know and I doubt that the best of them would stand translation into English. In Gaelic they were thrilling and picturesque, arousing either stark horror or merriment; but these effects were attained so subtly and depended so much on the nuances of Gaelic expression that they became dull and unconvincing in English. Many of them were a happy mixture of narration and verse, and almost all of them had jingles of some sort, jingles that resembled those of Mother Goose.

There was, of course, an art also in the telling of these tales, and experts in the telling, just as there were for the ghost stories. They, too, were a form of entertainment, and were popular on long winter nights. Some of the more simple people, and all of the children, doubtless believed every word of them; but most adults accepted them for what they were—just good stories.

No story was too fantastic to find some credence. Take for instant the story of the big snake that lived at Red Rory's rock. I sometimes passed this rock on the way to school, and never without trepidation. Some one reported seeing a large snake sunning itself by the rock. Later others reported seeing it. Each time the story was told the snake got bigger, as one storyteller outdid the other. The last time I heard it the snake was as big around as a flour-barrel, had eyes the size of a cup, and its coils disappeared into the woods some fifty yards away. For a finish what was probably a good-sized snake had been turned by imaginative people into Leviathan itself.

Grandfather liked to tell the story of the experience his grandfather had had with a mermaid; but this was in Scotland and not Cape Breton. His grandfather ran a sort of ferry between Barra and Glasgow, carrying occasional passengers back and forth, and freighting the products of the Island to Glasgow and returning with a cargo mostly of tea, cotton goods, and whiskey. One night he was sailing along alone through the seas of the North Atlantic on his way back to Barra, for he had no passengers. He got so tired in the long, dreary night that he fell asleep with the tiller in his hand.

He was awakened by the sweet voice of a woman, only to find his boat headed straight for the rocks of Staffa, and disaster. He quickly turned his boat, headed it in the right direction, and then looked about him for the source of the voice. He saw a mermaid, swimming along easily and gracefully in the wake of the boat. She was beautiful beyond the beauty of earthly women, with long golden hair, limpid and sparkling blue eyes, and full, rounded white breasts.

Grandfather's grandfather thanked her for her kindness and thereupon they had a long talk together in the moonlight over the water. It was in Gaelic, to be sure, for that is the language of nature and the one that its unspoiled creatures understand. Of course it is a great honor to talk to a mermaid, for they are full of wisdom and know all the things that mortal men do not know and sometimes cannot understand. Grandfather's grandfather made the best of his opportunity and plied the charming creature with questions, all of which she answered with open frankness.

As dawn neared, she suddenly said:

"You have asked me everything, except about egg-water."

With that she dived into the depths of the sea, and he never saw her again.

It should be explained here that "egg-water," that is the water used in the boiling of eggs, has long been a subject of dispute in Barra and also in Washabuckt, some contending that it should not be used for another purpose, and some that it had great benefits in other uses. As the mermaid did not explain the riddle, it probably remains just that to this day.

T HE RELIGION OF THESE PEOPLE was simple, yet deep, abiding and unquestioned. It was accepted naturally in youth like the facts of life and remained steadfast through the years. No one was so individualistic in a race of extreme individualism, or so belligerent in a race of belligerent men, that he or she did not feel the need of the church, and bow humbly before its mandates, and make some effort at honoring its moral code. Every one turned to the church in all the crises of life, and all found hope and consolation in its ministrations. All looked forward to a better and happier hereafter in Heaven.

The parish church was at Iona in those days, as it still is, at least nine miles distant over rough country roads. Yet all but the very young and the very old attended mass on Sundays, except in extreme winter weather. All drove that distance in buggies, or walked it, many fasting so that they might receive communion. Those who could not get to the church said the rosary, or other prayers, at home at the hour of the mass, so that they, too, felt that they were participating in the service. Once or twice yearly, and sometimes more often, the parish priest came to Washabuckt to hear confessions and to say mass for the aged; and he could be depended upon to come at the hour of death to prepare the departing soul to meet its Creator.

In my latter years there the community, with the encouragement of the parish priest, decided to build a chapel in Washabuckt; but the making of this decision brought a long and bitter argument. Father was in the center of it. He was at Grandfather's home vacationing and taking a look at his two growing sons; and he was eager, perhaps too eager, to help the good cause of religion in Washabuckt. So when a meeting of the parishioners was called in the school he and Grandfather attended, and I went along to see the fun.

The pastor presided and asked for ideas. Father at once took the floor. He offered the parish the outright gift of a site for the chapel on land he owned, a beautiful spot and ideally located. He also offered suggestions as to what the chapel should be and how it could be built.

It should be explained that Father was a building engineer, and had erected some of the most famous buildings in the United States from Boston to San Francisco, many of them still standing.

Father's generosity and enthusiasm only brought resentment among his Washabuckt kinsmen and neighbors, many of whom had long been jealous of his success and fame, and had never before had a chance to tell him and the world what they knew about building. So the argument started; and it waxed hot and furious. Father had all the information, all the logic, all the generosity; but the others had all the votes. They would have nothing to do with anything that Father proposed, no matter how good and reasonable it was.

For a finish they decided to buy a site opposite the Protestant graveyard—where Catholic ghosts could mingle with the Protestant ghosts—and they named a committee of three old codgers, who never had built so much as a chicken coop, to supervise the erection of the chapel.

Father took all this with considerable resentment at the time and was quite vocal about it; but later, when his temper had cooled, he decided to do all he could to help the project, for after all it was a chapel for God. So he was the first to go to the forest and cut timber for the chapel, twice the amount that was required of each parishioner, and was the first to go to a quarry and haul stone to the site for the foundation. He also made a cash gift to the good priest to help pay for the site. He evidently was sorry for the fuss he had made, and wanted to make amends.

The committee of three, however, was not so easily mollified, for had not their pride been slighted? The old codgers visited the site and stood before the pile of quarried stone that Father had placed there. The stone was a type of slate that scaled a bit. It had been frozen when Father had taken it from the quarry, and now in warmer weather it had thawed and was scaling, but was still exactly what was required. They looked at the stone a long time. They stroked their chins. They looked at one another. Then they condemned the stone that God had made, and Father had quarried.

That finished Father. He never tried to do anything further for the chapel or for Washabuckt, and the parish did not get the timber he had sent to the sawmill. The chapel was built without his ideas, or his help.

Years later the pile of condemned stone still stood beside the finished chapel for all to see, a monument to ignorance and spite.

CHAPTER SEVEN

Education by the Rod

LIKE MOST OTHER simple-living people, the natives of Washabuckt stressed wisdom rather than knowledge, action rather than thought, the will rather than the intellect: so they were not deeply concerned over formal education as such. There were two schools in the community, one in Lower Washabuckt and one in Upper Washabuckt, each with one overworked teacher, but the curriculum was definitely limited to the "Three R's." The child that had learned to read and write and to add, subtract and divide was felt to have acquired all the education that was needed and henceforth could be more usefully employed on the farm than in the school.

In fact few, if any, persons in the neighborhood had ever heard of higher mathematics, the physical and social sciences, and the classic literatures, or ever missed not knowing them. They had lived for centuries in Washabuckt and Barra without them.

The Washabuckter accepted his liberty and security as he accepted the cycle of the seasons. He accepted the church's explanation of his origin and of the Cosmos without question. He accepted the church's code of morals with equal faith, and, while he did not always honor it, his intentions at least were good. A few external things, and occasionally an idea, came along to disturb his complacency, like the telephone, the wireless, and the airplane, but not with enough force to cause him to delve more deeply into the problems of life, government and the hereafter. He learned more from the soil, the forest and the sea than he did in school.

In pioneer days only boys went to school, for only they were felt to need what a school could give. The girls were kept at home where they were taught by their capable mothers to be good wives and good mothers. In those days many of the girls spoke only Gaelic, and indeed many of the boys attending the schools had to learn English as a foreign tongue. In my time all the girls went to school but there as elsewhere they spent much of their time in giggling and shy flirtation. English then was the only language taught and spoken in the school, but it was an English that was mixed with Gaelic words and spoken with a Gaelic intonation.

The two Washabuckt schools were modest and simple to the point of crudeness and hardship. Each was a small, unpainted, one-story structure of boards and shingles weather-beaten outside and unfinished inside except for the unwashed wooden floor. The furnishings and equipment were in keeping with the building—board desks and benches for the children, a homemade desk and chair for the teacher on a dais, with a painted board blackboard. Dominating the interior of each school was an iron wood-burning stove with some logs beside it. The big, rusty, ungainly thing took hours of encouragement and nursing before it got hot and never in my experience did it heat the room to the point of comfort. The unwashed, opaque windows had no blinds or curtains and so far as I know could not be opened. Each school had one door, facing south, away from the northern storms.

In the long winter months the pupils crowded their

benches about the stove, still in their coats, wraps and mitts, and spent more time in rubbing their hands, stamping their feet, and poking the fire than in study. The walls did keep out the howling winds and the drifting snows, but the interior of the school was only a few degrees less frigid than the frost-bound landscape outside. Everything in the school was cold and drab and uninviting, so that education was a dreary and dismal experience; and only children of the north, born and raised in its rigorous climate and trained in hardihood, could survive a day's school in the late fall, the winter and the early spring. Yet few had colds or any other disease; for if the educational system did little for the minds of the scholars it did make for strong bodies. Certainly no child was petted and spoiled.

The primitive rod and the ruler maintained discipline. There were always a bunch of birch switches of varying thickness and at least one strong ruler on the teacher's desk beside the school bell. Light switches were used for the younger children and heavier ones for the bigger boys and girls. The switch was applied to the legs and back and the ruler to the extended palm. Sometimes the enraged teacher could not wait to obtain a switch or ruler; with his or her own knuckles he or she rapped the pupil on the head or gave the pupil a slap or two across the face.

None of these punishments was pleasant, but the ruler was resented and dreaded more than the others, for it was often a more humiliating experience. The boy or girl was required to hold out his or her open hand, palm up, while the teacher swung on it many times. Few could do it without whimpering or withdrawing the hand from contact with the ruler, which meant more strokes, and loss of "face" before the whole school. Not many could go through such a trial with dignity, and these children had their pride. They preferred pain to humiliation.

Older boys, and occasionally some of the older girls,

would break or steal the teacher's rods, and this was considered good sport; but strange to say, no one ever thought of doing away with the ruler. This was probably due to an inherent respect for property, for while the countryside abounded with birch switches one had to buy a ruler in the country store, and it might even mean a trip to Baddeck to get one, and of course the school ruler was the personal property of the teacher. Then a ruler was dressed wood, nicely marked and varnished, and cost five cents.

When the supply of switches disappeared mysteriously, which was not infrequently, the teacher would wait for the need for one and then send the offender out into the woods for a new stock, usually specifying the number and the sizes required. This always caused some merriment, especially if the current victim happened to be the one who had done away with the original supply. There would be more merriment when the first victim brought back delicate and strawlike switches that had been slashed so they would break under vigorous use. This would infuriate the teacher the more, and he would thereupon send out a new switch-gatherer, usually one of the teacher's pets, for switches adequate for their task. On rare occasions the teacher would have to leave the school to get a supply and this would mean a frolic in the school, which, however, would bring quick retribution.

Corporal punishment was taken for granted both by the pupils and their parents, and there was never any lasting resentment, although the beatings were never mild and sometimes harsh in the extreme. The use of the rod or ruler was accepted as a necessary part of education, as the whip was for the fractious colt. No teacher ever tried to impose discipline without punishment. The community believed that evildoing should not go unpunished; and even the pupil recognized the teacher's right to beat him for his shortcomings.

The pupil did not hold the beatings against the teacher, nor the teacher against the pupil, for they could be good friends outside the school. In fact, the teacher would go to great lengths to help the backward pupil who had been beaten again and again. Certainly, however, it did not make school an agreeable experience, nor encourage higher education. At that it was no worse than the discipline of Doctor Arnold at Rugby, which shortly before that time revolutionized the public schools of England.

The school was graded according to the six Royal Readers used in teaching reading. There were no examinations. The pupil moved from one reader to the other as he or she acquired proficiency in reading and when his or her parents could buy or borrow the next Reader. Few pupils ever went beyond the fourth Reader, which was considered in Washabuckt adequate ability to read, and the sixth Reader was considered higher education. In fact there were passages in the sixth that would confound some of the teachers, as well as words that he or she could not pronounce or explain. The child that mastered the sixth was believed to be a prodigy, and considered eligible to a clerkship in the neighborhood general store, to a job as a teacher, or even to aspire to the priesthood.

Memory was stressed in all school work. Months and in some cases years were devoted to memorizing the alphabet, forwards and backwards and crossways. The multiplication table was taught the same way. No one ever forgot either, if he or she lived to be one hundred years old. All the numerous poems and aphorisms in the Readers were learned by heart, as the saying went, and persons decades out of school could repeat them word by word. The same was true with spelling—there were no rules for spelling, just plenty of memory work.

Spelling bees in which the whole school participated were held about once a week. They were the highlights of the school term. Two team leaders would be named by the teacher and they in turn picked the members of their teams until the last child had a role. The teacher would call out the words and the fun would begin. The champion was soon known to the whole community, and could strut about for a week at least.

Memory work also entered the teaching of grammar, for the pupil had to be able to recite the eight parts of speech in exact order and the rules governing their use. No teacher that I encountered ever taught the relevancy of grammar to speech and I am not sure that they knew anything about it. One simply spoke a language as best one could, whether Gaelic or English, and let it go at that. Of course no one ever speaks two or more languages equally well, for one speaks his native tongue as perfectly as he can, and other languages as well as he can. The average Washabuckter butchered the English language both in pronunciation and syntax, and no one had any regrets about it, for it was an alien language anyway and not held to be a very good one at that.

The long walks to the school in the winter months were a trial that few of the pupils will ever forget. There were no heated busses to take them there and back home again. Each child had to fend for itself. Some had to trudge two or three or more miles each way through unbroken roads, sometimes hip-deep in snow banks and drifts and over treacherous ice hidden by the snow, while the cruel winds penetrated their scanty clothes. No child in my time had an overcoat, and not many had underwear. Cold hands and cold feet were accepted as normal. Yet no one complained, for no one knew anything better. But all looked forward to the spring, when the green grass would reappear, and the first flowers rise from the recently frozen ground, and the birds would again be busy making nests and laying eggs, and life would be a pleasant experience.

The teachers shared all the hardships of the pupils and had some extra ones of their own. Overworked and underpaid, they, too, had to walk back and forth to the school in all weathers and suffer many inconveniences. Besides, the teacher had to board on the community, for there was not enough cash available to make up a livable salary and they had to accept free board as part compensation. Then they were expected to help with the farm or household chores of the family they were visiting.

Thus the teacher would spend a week or more each term with each family in the school district, unless a family was too remote or too poor, eating with the family and sleeping in all kinds of beds. The teacher carried a small bag of clothes and never had a permanent room that he or she could call his or her own. While the food was always adequate it was sometimes coarse and poorly cooked, and in the winter the bed was cold, although in the most severe weather the blankets might be warmed before the fire or a heated stone placed in the bed to ease the rigors. Yet I have never known a teacher to complain and some of them seemed to enjoy the life, for it certainly was varied and they got to know every one in the community, young and old.

Teachers were respected for their position and for their knowledge. Their advice was sought on the larger problems of life and they were sometimes consulted on family affairs. Some of the less literate Washabuckters accepted their pronouncements with awe and were astounded by all they knew. Some actually believed the teacher knew all that was to be known; and that if the teacher did not, the parish priest did. Some teachers cultivated this idea, although their learning was limited and their vision circumscribed by their small experience; but others were more modest or more sensible and instead stressed the wide sweep of knowledge and how little any one could know.

Most families tried to do their best by the visiting teachers and to make them feel at home. The children always enjoyed having the teacher as a guest, for it meant better food and interesting discussions. All Washabuckters loved to talk. The teacher was always a guest of honor, and as such would be asked to lead the family in the saying of the rosary and other prayers, to propose a toast at a wedding, or to recite the litany for the dead at a wake. The teacher attended all the neighborhood frolics and shindigs and would sing with the singers and call the lancers and other popular square dances. The teacher was also welcomed for his or her store of gossip, for they knew more of the intimacies of the neighborhood than most others and were not averse to revealing them.

However, no teacher remained long in one of the Washabuckt schools, seldom more than one school year, but this was probably because other communities could pay them better.

The most interesting teacher in Washabuckt in my time, at least to me, was a Presbyterian minister without a church, who taught in the Upper Washabuckt school for one term—from January until June. His salary was reported to be $24 for that period, which was a record low, even for Washabuckt. He was not more than five feet tall and did not weigh more than one hundred pounds. He had a bald head and a whiskered face, except for a shaved chin and upper lip, which gave him the expression of a chimpanzee. He had a wobbling and shuffling gait like a sick duck, black, beady eyes and a meek manner that seemed an apology for living. There was much mystery about him and where he came from, and when the school term was over he disappeared as mysteriously as he had come.

Yet he was a man of great scholarship, one of the most learned I have ever met, anywhere. I was visiting Washabuckt at the time after two years in college and he loved to visit me to read my books. He could read my Homer in the original Greek and Virgil in the original Latin and he was familiar with all the philosophers from ancient Greece to modern times, and could discuss them and their doctrines with understanding and wisdom. In a moment of confidence he told me that he had done graduate work at Princeton University, and while there had fallen from a trapeze and injured his skull on the gymnasium floor. This I believe, and it probably explains everything. He had had churches, small ones in remote communities, but his eccentricities were too much even for them. He loved his Bible and could read it in the original Greek and Hebrew. He was a godly man.

His months in Washabuckt were a great trial to him, although he would not admit it, for he could not maintain discipline in the school. The pupils, old and young, boys and girls, ran riot. They paid no attention to his teaching; they would not answer his questions, and would come and go as they wished. Instead of doing their tasks the boys organized fights and played games, and the girls gossiped, and giggled at the pranks of the boys. He did not believe in corporal punishment and anyway did not have the physical strength to apply it. He appealed to them in every way he knew with the same dismal results. He finally tried bribery, although that was against his principles. He would visit the country store and from his almost empty pocketbook he would take ten cents. He would use that to buy candy and raisins for the children and cloves and snuff for himself, tiny portions, each in a paper bag. The pupils would take the proffered candy and raisins and then proceed to ignore him. Thus he carried on mildly but courageously until his term was over.

He was filled with the missionary spirit and, doubtless hoping that he could succeed with the elders where he had failed with the children, he organized temperance meetings at night in the school. He got me to preside at one of them. All of the rowdies of the neighborhood and their girl friends came to scoff. Bottles of whiskey were passed around ostentatiously while he was berating the demon of alcohol. With raucous, derisive voices the audience joined in singing his temperance hymns. And when he passed around the collection plate they dropped buttons and slugs on it. They laughed when they should weep and they applauded and cheered loudly and mockingly through his talks, and at the end. There were those present also who would have liked to listen to him with respect; but they never had a chance to do so. The old teacher never gave any indication that things were not as they should be—possibly because he knew more of the failings and weaknesses of his neighbors than they themselves did, and felt sorry for them.

The greatest indignity heaped upon him in Washabuckt, however, was when he was sent to visit Big Betsy, a riotous neighborhood character then in her nineties, who will have a later chapter for herself, because she deserves it. Some of these rowdies convinced her, which was not difficult to do, that the old minister was the antichrist, and they reveled in her eloquent and violent denunciations of the devil and all his works and especially his machinations in Washabuckt. Then some one got the idea of bringing Old Betsy and the teacher face to face, and all agreed that that would be great fun.

Other means failing, they sent the minister one morning to deliver a bottle of milk at her one-room cottage, where she lived alone. Meanwhile they followed him and hid behind trees so they could hear and see what happened. When the teacher opened the door of the cottage Old Betsy had just risen from bed and was stark naked. With a curse she grabbed an ax and made for him. He barely escaped from the cottage and she chased him across the countryside, brandishing the ax and hurling imprecations upon his innocent bald head. The hidden spectators were overcome with laughter, and did not recover their calm for days. It is a good thing that Old Betsy did not catch up with the minister, for that would have meant a terrible and shocking tragedy. The old minister never mentioned the matter, but he made certain never to encounter Old Betsy again.

The most respected teacher that Washabuckt had ever known was Michael B. MacDonald from St. Columba, a modest community in the mountain forests back of Washabuckt. He was known locally as Michael Fast, for every time he opened his mouth, which was often, a torrent of words poured out, one crowding upon the other as if he had too much to say and no time to say it. Actually he was a man of splendid character, wide knowledge and profound wisdom, and besides all this a great teacher, for he knew how to interest his pupils and to get them to learn. I had the good fortune to be with him for a year, and I learned more from him than I learned later in proud and noted preparatory schools and universities.

Michael Fast started his teaching career in a Washabuckt school while a mere boy and my Father was one of his first pupils. Father had a deep affection for him ever afterwards; and he made certain that my brother and I had a chance to benefit from his wisdom. So we were sent to board with a neighbor in St. Columba and attended the little school by a brook in the trees. Michael Fast could have had other and better schools; but his brother had lived nearby and had died leaving a poor widow and a flock of boys, and he, a bachelor, took over the burden of supporting and educating them. This was no light task, for one of the boys was blind and one a cripple and all were noisy and unruly and blessed with rapacious appetites. Michael Fast kept discipline in the home as he did in the school, but was always kind and patient. He had a big heart as well as an alert mind and rapid tongue. May his soul rest in peace!

GRANDFATHER ALSO INFLUENCED my early education. He understood the value of education and in this respect was far in advance of most of his neighbors. He made certain that my brother and I attended school every day and did our homework. No excuse, short of serious illness, was allowed to interfere. After trying many my brother and I decided that there was no way of avoiding school or evading the assigned tasks. He kept a close watch on us. He also encouraged us to read his books and his newspapers.

Grandfather was an omnivorous reader and, modest as it was, had the only thing that could be called a library in Washabuckt. He had English and Gaelic translations of the Bible. He had a dozen Gaelic song books, which were his pride and joy. He had a recent edition of *Whitaker's Almanac*, an abridged Webster dictionary, reports from the Nova Scotia Experimental Farm at Truro, histories of Scotland, Canada and Rome, some of Scott's novels, including *Rob Roy* and *Ivanhoe*, some of Dickens', including *David Copperfield* and *The Pickwick Papers*, and a miscellany of other books. He had a large map of North America pinned on the kitchen wall, which showed Canada and the United States in detail.

Grandfather subscribed to three newspapers, each costing a dollar a year. One was *The Casket*, the diocesan organ printed in Antigonish, and, then as now, well written, which kept him abreast of Catholic affairs and movements. Another was *The North Sydney Herald*, then as now the home journal of all natives of Eastern Cape Breton, which kept him informed on Cape Breton interests and events in neighboring communities. The third was *The Family Herald and Weekly Star*, the weekly edition of *The Montreal Star*, which gave a good outline of Canadian and world events and contained many interesting articles on the home and the farm, news of styles, cooking recipes, some fiction and a choice assortment of other reading. The mail came to Washabuckt three times a week and each delivery usually brought a newspaper for Grandfather. He would halt all other work until he had read his newspaper, and that meant reading every word of every column. Woe betide the person who interrupted or disturbed his reading!

Grandfather's reading influenced mine, for he always encouraged me to read good books, and I developed reading habits then that stay with me to this day. "A good book will talk to you like a wise friend," he would say. He recommended books to read, always ones that he himself had enjoyed.

Of the books in his small library, *Whitaker's Almanac* proved the most interesting to me and made the most lasting impression on my young mind. I had great curiosity about the great, outside world, and it gave me the kind of exact information that I needed. From it I learned the highest mountains, the longest rivers, the busiest harbors, the biggest cities, the population of the great nations, the areas of the various countries and continents, the tallest buildings, the crops and industrial output of the world, the men and women then ruling all peoples, sports records, and a vast fund of facts that were a wide education in themselves, and proved valuable later in life, and especially in my work as a journalist. I still feel that *Whitaker's Almanac* or *The World Almanac* or similar books of exact facts should be in every boy's collection of books—and in every girl's also, for that matter. Besides giving a boy or a girl valuable information they train him or her in exactness.

Grandfather's own reading was often punctuated with outbursts. The world was going to Hell then also, although, as usual, it did not get there. In any case he did not like things as they were and could be quite indignant about them. I often wondered why he read about events that were bound to upset him; but he obviously enjoyed both his reading and his outbursts.

During the Boer War his sympathies were all with

the Boers. Grandfather would expatiate on the many virtues and the great capabilities of Oom Paul and his generals and excoriate the British General, Sir Hector MacDonald, who, of course, was a good Scot and had risen from the ranks. Grandfather thought him a real man. He particularly resented the use made of the Scottish regiments and their heavy casualties; and insisted that the English always put the Scots in the danger spots and made them win all the costly victories. One of his pet theories was that the English got other peoples, especially the Scots and the Irish, to do the fighting for them.

Grandfather could be equally vociferous and indignant over events nearer home. He did not like Sir Charles Tupper and his policies as Prime Minister of Canada; and when Sir Wilfrid Laurier succeeded him as Prime Minister he condemned the new government and its policies with the same virulence. He loved lost causes and impossible ones. He remained a confirmed Jacobite long after every one else had abandoned the Stuart cause as hopeless. He spoke kindly of Bonnie Prince Charlie, despite his many failings, all of which he knew, and loved to sing his praise in Gaelic songs.

He wanted to understand everything he read about, but there were some things he could not understand. Marconi's new Atlantic wireless was one of these. The Italian inventor in those days had set up a station at Glace Bay in Cape Breton, and *The North Sydney Herald* and *The Family Herald and Weekly Star* had long reports of his doings. The more Grandfather studied the news reports the more convinced he became that what Marconi pretended to do just could not be done. Finally he consulted Crooked Dan, who claimed to know everything about it. They had many long and heated conferences. They concluded that Marconi had got his messages across the Atlantic; but they refused to admit that he had done so without a wire or some other physical link.

Dan put forth the theory that Marconi's instruments could throw a ball of electricity for great distances—something like a bolt of lightning—and insisted that he must have had a relay of anchored ships that would toss this electric ball one to the other over the vast expanse of ocean. Grandfather did not accept this theory; but he could offer no better solution. Grandfather continued to feel that Marconi was a faker.

I was witness to another conference between Grandfather and Crooked Dan on a scientific problem.

An eclipse of the sun took Washabuckt by surprise one afternoon, much like the one at the Court of King Arthur that gave the Connecticut Yankee his great opportunity. As the ghastly, unearthly light descended on the countryside the birds flew with startled cries for their homes in the forest, the cattle left the pasture and headed for the barn, Rory, the dog, bayed anxiously at the strange scene, and Grandfather stood in a field contemplating the celestial spectacle in silence. Just then Dan hove into sight, riding down the road in his buggy.

Grandfather hailed Dan, who stopped the horse, and limped to where he was standing. A minute later Grandmother, her prayer beads in her hand, joined them.

"What can it be, Dan?" Grandfather asked his learned neighbor.

For answer Crooked Dan turned to Grandmother and ordered her to bring him a silk handkerchief. He unfolded it without a word, and then with solemn dignity moved to a nearby picket fence. He stooped behind the fence so that he lined up two stakes with the sun, and holding the handkerchief before him with both hands he gazed through it for some minutes, maybe five minutes, but it seemed interminable. The quiet was appalling and ominous as we waited for the momentous decision.

At last he walked back, folded the handkerchief deliberately and handed it back to Grandmother, and then turned to Grandfather and announced:

"Michael Eoin, my good friend, you are the witness to an apocalyptic scene. I thought at first that Judgment Day was at hand. But it ain't so! It ain't so! Not yet!"

With that he limped again to his buggy, lifted himself into it and drove off without another word. Grandfather smiled, but said nothing.

MEANWHILE EPOCH-MAKING experiments were being made over the water of the Lake in the summers and over the ice in the winters, but the people of Washabuckt, although knowing them, paid them little heed. No one bothered to go out and look at them. The teachers and the children in the schools took no note of them; in fact, they were probably not mentioned in school. I happened to be present at several of them, more by chance than by design.

Alexander Graham Bell, the Scot who invented the telephone and made a fortune out of it, bought Red Head for a summer estate. This was a point of land that jutted into the water about five miles across the lake from Grandfather's farm, and rose abruptly into a beautiful mountain. He renamed it "Beinn Bhreagh," which in Gaelic means "beautiful mountain." On this property he built a garish and massive home of Victorian architecture, an observation tower near the peak of the mountain, and some laboratories. There the aging inventor lived for many years; and there he is buried.

Reports reached Washabuckt that he had dug a tunnel into the mountain into which he would retreat to think and study in complete quiet. The natives never understood why one should need such protection from the world, but they were ready to believe anything they heard about Professor Bell, no matter how fantastic; that is, after he had sent emissaries to see their flocks of sheep.

The great inventor had plans for improving the breed

of sheep in the neighborhood. He got the idea that a sheep might as well have three or four lambs as one or two. It would be the same trouble to the sheep and that much more profitable to the farmer. So he sent men through the surrounding countryside to locate ewes that had multiple births, and in the absence of these, ewes with more than two teats.

When these experts reached Washabuckt and proceeded to count the teats of the sheep, the Washabuckters, who knew nothing of the great inventor's intentions, decided that he was completely daft.

So when there were strange doings over the Lake the Washabuckters took it for granted that Professor Bell had got another brilliant idea, and let it go at that. The fact was that the old man was interested in flying. He had gathered some able and daring young men about him to carry out his ideas and to contribute their own. Among them was Glenn H. Curtiss, who brought the "Silver Dart," one of the most famous of the early airplanes, to "Beinn Bhreagh" with him.

Doctor Bell felt that moderate speed and not high speed was the key to successful flying, as being safer and more reliable. So he developed a large man-carrying kite named the "Cygnet," made up of a mass of cells through which the air poured. This kite was towed from the stern of a speedboat and rose to a height of 168 feet over the Lake. But it was not the success that had been hoped for and later it was abandoned. Bell and his associates continued their experiments with the airplane. They built a new model on the lines of the "Silver Dart," and this Curtiss, J.A. Douglas McCurdy, and Frederick W. ("Casey") Baldwin flew with varying success.

These were historic days although the people of Washabuckt did not realize it, for these were the earliest heavier-than-air flights in the British Empire, and these young men were the forerunners of the boys who thirty years later saved the Empire and the civilized world in the Battle of Britain. I saw some of these first uncertain flights that were fraught with so much danger and so much hope. I was present when the airplane rose to the height of 150 feet and set a new altitude record. That was a great day!

However, the people of Washabuckt should not be censured for ignoring the historic flights off their shores. They only did what Americans did when the Wright brothers made their famous flights at Kitty Hawk. Human flight was incredible in those days, and it still seems so to me after numerous flights over great distances.

While the Washabuckters certainly did not overemphasize education, the education that they acquired was obviously all that was required for their simple needs. As I said at the beginning of this chapter, they stressed wisdom rather than knowledge, and they had a wisdom that could not be obtained in schools.

CHAPTER EIGHT

Three Boys in the Country

THE FREE, OPEN LIFE of the country is the ideal life for a boy. He lives close to nature as God intended boys to live. He is one of the crops of the farm along with the hay, the potatoes, and the grain, and one of the farm animals along with the horses, the cows and the poultry. He knows the sun and the moon and the stars and he can dream. He knows the cycle of the seasons and each brings its special chores and pleasures. He develops a healthy body and a clear mind. Perhaps the city is more stimulating after he has reached maturity, but there can be little doubt that the grown man is the better for having spent his youth close to the soil. Few who have had the experience regret it. I never have.

The companionship of other boys is as necessary to full enjoyment of life in the country as it is in the city. A boy needs other boys to share his adventures and his duties. Three make the best team, just enough and not one too many or one too few. Three can thrill together in the brave adventure or the new experience and three can be miserable together when retribution must be faced in the form of a stern grandfather.

There were three of us boys together in Washabuckt

in these days, and summer and winter we got into many scrapes and explored the countryside, the mountain, the Lake. When one could not suggest some form of mischief the other could, and did. This team included my younger brother Murdoch, known in the neighborhood as Murdoch Beag, or Little Murdoch, although he grew to be six feet four inches tall, and my cousin Murdoch, sometimes known as Murdoch Bàn, or blond or pale Murdoch, but more commonly as Murdoch Mór, or Big Murdoch, for he was a year or two older than my brother and at the time bigger physically.

The three of us were inseparable pals, and the only restraint on us was the inflexible will of Grandfather, who was now nearing eighty. We found many ways of evading or misinterpreting his orders so that we tried his patience to the point of despair. Over and over again he predicted that all three of us would end in the penitentiary, if not on the gallows.

Grandfather had firm faith in the rod in the bringing up of boys. He kept an ample supply of switches at all times and made full use of them. Daily he quoted the Biblical injunction: "He that spareth the rod hateth his son." This was probably in self-justification, for he was a man of deep affection for his family as well as the dispenser of inflexible discipline. We had more evidence of his severity than his love and we were astounded to discover one day that he had been bragging about his three grandsons. On our part we admired the Old Gentleman as much as we feared him.

Each of us took his beatings from Grandfather differently, for each of us had his own idea of how to ease the misery. As the oldest and the biggest and generally considered the leader and chief mischief-maker I was always thrashed first. From the first stroke I would wail loud and long. Big Murdoch tried to keep out of sight in the hope that the Old Man would forget about it, or at least that the worst of his rage would pass. It never did him any good, although at times he missed Grandmother's good meals. When the beating did catch up with him Big Murdoch would strive to outdo me in wailing and bawling, which was not easy and did him no good either. Little Murdoch would never utter a sound, no matter how hard and long he was beaten. He doubtless took the worst beatings of all. They were certainly the least satisfactory so far as Grandfather was concerned.

One day we three boys had a conference in the barn on the best tactics to use with Grandfather when he was bent on chastisement. The beatings were coming too often and were too severe to suit us. I argued that my tactics were the best. The two Murdochs agreed to try them.

Within the week Grandfather found it necessary to whip all three of us, one after the other. Everything went according to form until he hit Little Murdoch across the back with the rod. Thereupon the loudest and most unearthly howls ever heard in Washabuckt rent the neighborhood calm. Little Murdoch had been rehearsing for the occasion and had learned the role well.

Grandmother dropped her work and came rushing to the scene. The dog started to bark. The cat slithered into the tall grass to hide. The hens in the barnyard screamed and scattered and sought cover, thinking a hen-hawk or the end of the world was at hand. The cows stopped chewing their cud and looked wonderingly about. A neighbor driving along the road stopped the horse and stood up in the buggy to get a better view.

Grandfather stopped the beating abruptly, rod in mid-air. He examined the rod, then he examined Little Murdoch. Big Murdoch started to snicker. I could not forbear a smile. Grandfather quickly realized he was being tricked and he resumed the beating. Little Murdoch received a half-dozen extra strokes for good measure.

From then on we returned to our old separate ways

of dealing with such unpleasant occasions.

The thrashings should not be overemphasized, for they had only a minor part in the life of three happy boys. They were accepted as part of the price one had to pay for the enjoyment of many happy experiences. They did not restrain us in the least. They did not come more than once every week or two. Meanwhile we would have lots of fun. We could do many things that Grandfather would not discover and sometimes Grandmother would intervene and save us. But a beating was always in the background, and had to be considered in most things we enjoyed doing.

As we grew older and bigger we came to have a fine understanding of Grandfather's sense of justice and the consequences in retribution of most adventures. Moreover, as Grandfather also got older the beatings became more of a trial to him than to us, so that more and more he would let us off with a scolding. In the later years we would stop and weigh the consequences before violating his orders and determine whether it meant a beating or a scolding and whether it was worth one or the other, or perhaps both. Usually we decided to have our adventure regardless of the result. Actually the beatings added the spice of uncertainty and intrigue to our lives.

Then there were the farm chores. These were numerous at some times of the year and generally a bother to three boys at all times, but they were done as a part of life and living, something that every boy had to do and would be a shirker if he did not do. Work never ends about the home and barns of the farm, especially one that has no modern facilities and is dependent entirely on manpower and horsepower, as was the situation in Washabuckt. Usually, however, the chores did not take much time, not with three of us to do them, and we had an abundance of time left for mischief.

We had to find the cattle in the pastures on the mountain and drive them to the barnyard for milking. We had to cut the firewood into stove lengths, split it, and stack it in the kitchen. We had to carry bucket after bucket of water from the well to the home and the barn. In the spring we had to help with the repairing of the fences and the planting; in the summer with the hoeing of the potatoes and turnips and the making of the hay; and in the fall with the harvesting of the crops and the plowing. In the winter we had to help feed and water the stock, curry the horses and clean the stables. After supper each evening we had to wash the dishes for Grandmother.

There were other chores that we considered more fun than work.

We loved to go into the forest with the men after the first heavy snow to fell the big trees for the year's firewood. The logs were then hauled out over the snows in the roadless woods by horse-sled. It was great sport to topple over the aged maples, beeches and birches with a magnificent crash. It was also good sport to study and to trace the tracks of birds and animals in the fresh, soft snow. We might see a fox, or an otter, or a rabbit, and as we generally carried a gun we might come home with a partridge or a rabbit for supper. The forest itself was a picture to stir the imagination of an impressionable boy, with the evergreens, the spruces, the firs, the pines and the hemlocks, bent down under their heavy burden of white, and the other trees standing naked, cold and solemn in the deep stillness. The air was a tonic for body and soul. Clear, light and crisp when inhaled it delighted the nostrils with a frosty tickle. Exhaled, it became a cloud of vapor.

Another treat was fishing with Grandfather, who was strictly utilitarian, merely seeking food for his family's table and not considering the getting of it sport. He used either a net or a spear. He did, however, enjoy seeing the fun we got out of it and always asked us to join him.

On evenings, after the day's work, when Grandfather

announced that he was going to set the net in the Lake, the three of us would let out wild whoops and dash ahead of him to the shore to prepare the boat and the net. When he arrived he would take his position in the stern with the net and we would laboriously row the boat to the chosen spot in the Lake. Grandfather would cast an anchor to hold the net fast and then pay out the sixty or more yards of it. Cork floats would be bobbing along the surface of the water while the rest of the weighted net slowly sank to the bottom. Early next morning we would take up the net and gasp in wonder at all the marvels of the deep that had been caught in its toils. These might include trout, eels, herring, tommycods, starfish, crabs, lobsters, flounders, perch, and if we were very lucky a salmon or a cod. We would return home in triumph with our catch and share it with our neighbors.

On summer days when the waters of the Lake were calm Grandfather would occasionally invite us to join him in spearing eels. Again we would row the boat, slowly and silently, while the Old Man, even when past eighty, would stand erect and confident in the bow with his long spear in hand and his keen eyes scanning the bottom of the Lake.

When he saw an eel lying on the sand or moving slowly among the eelgrass, he would gently move the spear in its direction until just above it and then impale it with a sudden lurch. I never knew him to miss one. His aim was deadly.

When we were older we were allowed to spear eels at night by ourselves. We needed calm waters, and we attached a home-made wire basket to the bow of the boat in which we burned birch bark to illumine the waters. It was a thrilling experience in the stygian darkness and we saw, or imagined we saw, all sorts of monsters in the waters and strange forms in the night. We always got plenty of eels.

We also speared eels through the ice in the winter, using a steel spear of many prongs made by the local blacksmith. Soon after the ice formed on the Lake most of the men of the neighborhood would gather on the ice over a spot on the Lake about two miles from our shore, where the bottom was muddy and the eels hibernated. Each man would cut a hole in the ice and from it drive the spear into the mud in all directions. Soon the ice would be covered with squirming or frozen eels.

OUR GREATEST ADVENTURES with Grandfather, however, were our monthly cruises across the Lake to Baddeck to market the produce of the farm and to bring back provisions for the home. Baddeck, the county seat, with three or four general stores, four churches, a telegraph and telephone office, two hotels, a high school, and fewer people than some Bronx tenements, was the trading and cultural center of the neighboring communities. As a village it was simple, clean and innocent, but for us boys it seemed the ultimate in sophistication and abandon, for Washabuckt men went there to drink as well as to trade and the women bought things that they concealed from their menfolk. The journey of four miles was made by boat in the summer and over the ice by horse and sleigh in the winter.

It took days for us to prepare for the trip, especially if Grandmother were planning to go with us. Grandfather would gather produce to take along, perhaps new potatoes and a lamb or two, and Grandmother would take butter and eggs, and possibly some chickens. For days Grandfather would scan the winds and the clouds, the sunsets and the sunrises, the moon and the stars, for he was his own weather forecaster, and he was seldom wrong. There would be an air of expectancy and adventure about the farm that even Rory the dog could sense, and that seemed to cause things to go wrong. Sometimes this air of suspense would pervade the neighborhood, for people seemed to know about the contemplated trip without being told about it.

With the weather propitious, we would start early in the morning of the appointed day. The produce would be carted to the shore and stowed carefully in the boat, a twelve-foot, homemade argosy, waterproofed and weighed down from constant tarring, with two oars and a tiny tan sail, that moved ponderously through the waters with the greatest reluctance. Grandfather would sit at the tiller, master of the situation and adequate for any emergency. Grandmother and we three boys would sit where and how we could. If the wind was fair we would hoist our mast and spread our sail; if not we boys would take to the oars and pull and puff and splash in the direction of Baddeck. We would be on our way with courage and hopes that would have done credit to Jason in the *Argo* in his quest for the golden fleece.

While Grandfather and Grandmother would be doing their marketing we would explore Baddeck. We would admire the motorboats and sleek yachts of the summer visitors from the United States; examine all the goods in the stores, especially the guns and fishing gear; study longingly and avariciously the displays of candy and sweets; and always end up with a dish of ice cream each. On occasions the Baddeck boys taunted us, and it gave us vast pleasure to mess up their neat clothes, straight from the T. Eaton & Co. catalogue, in the dusty streets. They soon learned to leave us alone. Altogether the visits to Baddeck were worth the tremendous effort.

The most memorable visit to Baddeck, however, was not made by us or any of our kin, but by Little Rory the Big Tailor, the most intemperate man in Washabuckt. It was the early spring and the ice on the Lake was treacherous, but as his home was short of supplies his wife allowed him to take a load of produce to Baddeck. Over and over again she cautioned him not to look at a bottle, but to sell the produce, buy what was needed and come right back home. Her admonitions only served further to whet Little Rory's already prodigious thirst.

Little Rory arrived at the market all right and disposed of his produce, but instead of taking goods in trade he took cash. Then he tied his horse to a hitching post and proceeded to do the town. He bought a bottle of whiskey and soon disposed of it with the help of some willing friends. Then he emptied another. With the last of the money he bought a third. Then he finally decided to head for home.

Meanwhile it had started to rain. Soon it was a raging torrent driven by a full gale. The snow on the roads turned to slush. Huge pools of water, and some say cracks, appeared on the ice. Afoot Little Rory sloshed and slopped and staggered and weaved his way across the Lake, wet, cold, hungry and drunk, at times roaring Gaelic songs into the face of the wind and at others halting to challenge the champions of the world to come forth to do him battle.

Some hours later he reached his farm. He went direct to the stable. There he brushed down one of his warm and comfortable cows and tied a blanket securely about her. That done he sneaked into his home and to bed so silently that his worried wife did not hear him.

The next morning the ice was broken and there were large areas of open, green water on what had been the frozen Lake. It took Little Rory a month to recover his horse and sleigh. They were brought to Washabuckt by ferry.

NOT MANY OF THE CHORES of the farm, however, were a delight to three high-spirited boys bent on other things; on the contrary most of them were dreary drudgery. On top of the list of dull, monotonous tasks I would put stone-picking, which seems to harass boys on farms the world over. I have yet to meet any one who enjoyed it.

There were always large fields to clear of stones on Grandfather's farm, usually fields brought back to hay after being plowed for other crops. Every year there were new fields to pick; and it will probably be so to the end of time.

If you could pick one stone crop and be done with it you would have had the satisfaction of having done a job, unpleasant though it might have been; but a few years later after a fresh plowing there would be a new crop of stones on that field. We could not figure out where all the stones came from. Little Murdoch suggested that it might be the work of some evil spirit. We took the problem to Grandfather and for once he, too, was stumped. After several days of cogitation he finally expressed the opinion that the stones were pushed to the surface by successive frosts and thaws. This explanation seems more plausible now in retrospect than it did then to his three stone-pickers.

We tried several schemes to turn stone-picking from drudgery to fun, but without much success. Instead of putting them one by one into a basket and lugging them to a central pile on the edge of the field or on some waste land, we set up a target on the desired assembly spot and hurled them at it. This we soon discovered meant picking them over and over again and prolonged the agony. We tried to make it a competitive sport; that is, to see who could pick the most in the shortest time; but this we found was only another way of fooling ourselves. We tested other ideas, but our final decision was that there was only one way of picking stones, and that was to pick them.

Picking potato bugs, when one would be much happier swimming in the Lake, was another form of torture; and a task that supplied another mystery. We could never figure out how those miserable and dumb bugs could discover every potato patch in Washabuckt. They did.

No matter where the field was located the bugs would find it. In the spring when Grandfather was planning the crops we would ask him to place a potato patch here or there in some isolated area to fool the bugs, and once or twice he laughingly agreed to do so. But when the plants had reached the proper growth the bugs would be there by the thousand and we would have to pick them off the leaves and drop them into tins. We concluded that the bugs must have had spies about the neighborhood to report every potato field to a potato-bug headquarters.

As three boys alone with nature we had our greatest fun. Winter and summer there was always something interesting for us to do; and there were few things that a boy could do that we did not do. The changing seasons added variety to our lives, for each season brought a new countryside and its own special delights. No season lasted long enough to tire of it. We had a way of enjoying everything. Thus we could thrill to the autumnal storms on the Lake as we could revel in its placid, glass-like, summer calms. A normal, healthy, zestful boy can teach any psychiatrist lessons on how to adjust oneself to life.

The Lake was a constant source of fun for us. In winter it offered skating, sleigh-riding, fishing, seal hunting, and occasionally horse-racing on its icy surface. In the fall it offered duck-hunting. In the summer it provided swimming, boating, fishing, clamming, and yacht-racing. Besides we loved to watch the trading steamers and schooners, and were always present when one of them docked at the nearby Washabuckt wharf.

The mountain was also kind to us and a great source of joy. It was always an invitation for a stroll through the woods where we felt close to the birds and the animals that made it their home. Then we could set snares for rabbits; hunt partridge with homemade bow and arrow; search for bird nests, especially the rookeries of the crows, and the aeries of the eagles, and seek out the burrows of the foxes. And, when it was covered with snow and ice, we set traps for fox, mink, otter or ermine.

Our third playground was a large stream that flowed from the mountain into the Lake through a deep gulch and over rocks that made rapids, tumbling falls, and deep, dark, mysterious pools. Many trout dwelt in its rushing waters and whirling pools; and where it entered the lake there were smelts also. We loved to catch the trout and the smelts, light a fire, and make a meal of them on the spot. Sometimes we brought a dozen or more of them home to the family. We loved to swim in the cool water of the pools; but mostly we explored the strange twistings and wanderings of the stream up the mountainside.

Grandfather's farm with its hayfields, growing crops, pastures and barns also offered an infinite variety of experience; but when free we never lingered long about the farm, for Grandfather or Grandmother would be sure to find something for us to do.

On the whole we found nature benevolent and generous; but we also learned that it could be cruel. I shall never forget the time we found a large snake swallowing a frog. The snake was lying on a sunny rock in the stream. It paid no attention to us as we approached; and it was taking its time disposing of the frog. We killed the snake with a stone and freed the frog, which still had enough life in it to plunge into the dark waters of a nearby pool and vanish with two or three lunges. We were disappointed that it did not halt a moment to show its gratitude in whatever way it could. But then it was probably in a panic, for seldom does any animal face such a terrible fate and escape so fortuitously. We learned early that often one animal lives on another. It was a shock to us.

OUR SUPREME JOY was to slip off by ourselves, with nowhere in particular to go and nothing in particular to do but just to meander through the fields and the woods without seeking the pleasures that would soon come. Or we might just lie on our backs among the flowers and the grass and the sweet scents of a remote field on the farm or a clearing in the forest and idly and lazily gaze into the blue of the heavens or watch the white, fleecy clouds drift slowly by. Or we might pick and eat our fill of luscious wild berries, strawberries on some hillside, or raspberries along a fence or on the edge of the woods. We might spend hours daydreaming.

No one can understand a boy, or life either, who has not done his share of daydreaming, and sorry, indeed, is his lot. For youth is the time of hopes and visions when a vague castle in the air can be more real and more important than an ivy-clad pile of ancient rock overhanging the Rhine. These daydreams are so capricious and fleeting that it is difficult later to remember what they were or if any of them were realized. Yet the progress of mankind is the fruit of the daydreams of boys and girls down through the ages until at last they merge into the visions and aspirations of the present. From them have come the epic poems, the beautiful cathedrals, the sublime paintings, the great music, the new sciences, the philosophies, in fact all that has carried mankind on to better and higher things. They are the origin of our saints and scholars. Without them we would have remained savages in some tropical jungle.

My favorite spot for daydreaming was in the shade of a poplar tree on a hill overlooking the Lake. From there I could see the sails of the boats, several tree-covered islands, and the hazy, distant shores. The field about was populated with a profusion of daisies, buttercups, and other wild flowers and myriads of ants, grasshoppers, bees, wasps and other insects. A family of robins kept house in the poplar and other birds were frequent visitors to its branches. Here one could hear the soft, low music of nature; and the blended scents of the forest and meadow soothed the soul.

I liked to be alone with my dreams, but I was seldom without a visitor, a big, lazy, field fly, which I came to know well and to name "Billy." He was always welcome, for he was a friendly fly and made a boon companion. He respected my moods and seemed to sense the proper time to make an appearance. First he would soar about me in wide circles singing a merry song. He had quite a repertory, a song for every occasion and for every mood. Then he would approach me with confidence, usually sitting on my bare knee so that I could see and admire the purple splendor of his coloring. Finally he would perch himself on my nose and look into one of my eyes. He never tarried long, for he knew that I was there to dream, and he did not want to outstay his welcome.

The sophisticated people of the large cities do not know flies; at least they do not know enough to discriminate among them. They only know the house fly, the *musca domestica*, a species that was scarce, if not unknown, in Washabuckt in my time, and they treat all flies alike. This is probably due to the adverse propaganda of scientists and physicians, who have been preaching for decades that a fly is a germ-carrier and a pest, and who have never tried to cultivate the friendship of a decent fly. So they swat every fly within reach. No wonder flies do not like them.

In Washabuckt a fly was respected as one of God's creatures and allowed to live out its normal life. Later I was to learn that scientists and physicians also inform us that every man and woman are loaded to capacity with all kinds of germs and bacteria; yet I have never seen anybody going about swatting men and women as pests, although there is as much reason for swatting some of them as there is for swatting flies. Personally I suspect that a man is more liable to infect a fly than a fly is to infect a man. I commend this to the research departments of our universities as a subject worthy of thorough inquiry. Certainly I found "Billy" a model of cleanliness and a right decent and interesting fellow.

My daydreaming fired my imagination and brightened my life. I would give much today to be able to relive the rapture of those boyish dreams; but that is impossible. I have lived too long; I have seen too much; I have suffered too much. A mature man would be great if he could mix the dreams of his boyhood with his experience, and a boy would be a genius if he could add the experience of maturity to his dreams.

All that I can remember of my boyhood dreams, and that only vaguely, is that I intended to write a great epic poem in roaring, searing, melodious, flowing Gaelic measures that would stir the soul of humanity. I had been deeply impressed by a saying quoted by Grandfather, that if he could write the songs of a nation he did not care who wrote its laws. I decided there and then to write those songs. The fact that only a few could read my Gaelic verses did not disturb me. Gaelic-speaking Washabuckt was then my world, and that was enough.

Later my day-dreaming embraced all kinds of literature, leaping nimbly from one to the other. In those days I read several of the Scott novels, including *Ivanhoe* and *Rob Roy*, and in turn I was the hero of each novel or another Sir Walter Scott. One week I would be a strong, silent knight going about the world fighting for lost causes and doing good, and the next I would be a new Rob Roy, the terror of the neighborhood, and an invincible swordsman. Still later I would dream of writing thrilling novels of courageous heroes and beautiful but wronged women. Those I intended to be anonymous, a secret that I hoped to carry to my grave, so that all future ages would be left to speculate on who the great, popular writer was, and why he did not want his name known. Actually I started one of these great novels, but my resolution only carried me through one chapter.

As I got older my dreams turned to journalism, in terms of *The Victoria News*, *The North Sydney Herald* and *The Family Herald and Weekly Star*. In these my ideas were stimulated by Grandfather, who often spoke of how newspapers brought information from the far corners of the earth to their readers so that they might know the truth. In my boyish dreams I was the spotless champion of humanity, visiting the great of all nations, and attending all important events, extracting the truth and giving it to the millions waiting on my efforts. It seemed a noble and worthy cause; and it is.

About this time I was appointed the Washabuckt correspondent of *The Victoria News*. Weekly I gathered local personal items and mailed them to the editor; for which I got no pay but the honor and the experience. I shall never forget the thrill of seeing my first efforts in type. I was also thrilled by the fame and dignity my writing brought me in the community. Perhaps journalism was in my blood; anyway it became my life's work.

We three boys liked to share our dreams. We would discuss them among ourselves and commend them or find fault with them. We also had some dreams in common.

On a clear summer's day, with a smart breeze over the waters, we would watch the boats and ships sailing over the Lake and dream that one of them was ours. We needed a big boat of our own in the worst way. With it our dreams would be realized, for we could go sailing into strange seas and to exotic lands, where we would see many kinds of peoples and vegetation and meet with weird adventures. When a schooner would come tacking against the wind so that its sails obscured its deck we would run up on the shore and we could take possession of it. Some did come near the sands where we were waiting expectantly; but every last one had a captain and crew able to guide it and just when our hopes were highest it would turn suddenly with much flapping of sails and put out again into the Lake. Although we were disappointed over and over again we were never discouraged, for our hopes were infinite and eternal and we felt certain that the very next boat to come our way would be ours.

We never did get our boat and so we never started on our supreme adventure. But Big Murdoch did try to realize his dreams, for when he came to manhood he took to the sea and has sailed the waters of the seven seas ever since. To this day I receive letters and souvenirs from him sent from faraway ports in the Pacific and the Atlantic. The realization, however, is never quite what the dream envisioned. It never is.

Frequently we would climb the highest peaks of the Washabuckt mountains and then climb the highest tree we could find. There we would sit for hours like three birds on a limb, and gaze in admiration at the sight unfolded before us, the tree tops in the valleys, the farms at the edge of the Lake, the far-reaching arms of the Lake, the green fields and homes on the distant shores, and the misty blue mountains on the far horizons. We could see Baddeck with all its enticements, Beinn Bhreagh with Alexander Graham Bell's home and its modern civilization, and a wide panorama of Gaelic culture. Here were spread before us the beauty and majesty of what is considered by many the most magnificent scenery in Cape Breton, and by that token the most magnificent in eastern America, if not the world. It was a sight never to be forgotten; and it impressed us deeply. This was our world and we loved it. This was our happy adventure, and we never tired of it. This for the time satisfied our wanderlust.

Then the long, slow journeys through the woods going and coming were always interesting and rarely failed to produce an adventure. The most memorable was the time we walked right into a rookery. We discovered its location from the loud and distressful cawing of the colony of crows.

We determined to look into one of their nests. We picked the easiest tree to scale. Dozens of crows dashed down at us as we did so until they almost hit us and until there was danger that they might pick out our eyes; but we were not to be scared that way. In a few minutes what seemed like hundreds of crows made the heavens hideous with their croaking. We could scarcely hear one another speak from the noise. We finally reached the nest and in it we found three young ones. We decided to make pets of them.

Grandfather and Grandmother were disturbed when we returned home that evening with our three crows. They evidently knew more about crows than we did. They refused to allow us to have them in or near the house, but they did allow us to make a nest for them in a half-barrel in the barn. There we made them as comfortable as we could and set about feeding them. We soon learned that that was quite a task. They gulped down all the worms and grubs we could find, and demanded more, until there seemed to be no limit to their capacity. We named them Tom, Dick, and Harry, regardless of sex.

In a couple of weeks they grew too big for the nest and began to move about. First they explored the barnyard and caused consternation among the poultry. They seemed to delight in stealing the food from the hens and the ducks. The big red rooster resented their presence and chased them about, but they were too quick and too adroit for him. Later they found their way to the house, explored all parts of it, helped themselves to what they wanted, and messed things up. Still later they flew all over Washabuckt, entering barns and homes, and returning with bright objects, like scissors and cutlery, and with balls of yarn—all of which later had to be returned to their owners. In fact they became neighborhood pests.

From the start they were real pets for us boys, and the most interesting we ever had. They would fly to meet us on our return from school and perch on our shoulders or heads. They would take food from our mouths. They would follow us about the farm. They showed affection for us in every way they could. They did everything but talk, and soon we hoped to have them do that, for one of the neighbors informed us that a crow could talk if its tongue were split. We had about decided to do that, when we returned from school one day to find them missing.

Grandfather explained that they had heard the call of the wild and had simply flown away. But we suspected, probably correctly, that he had done away with them in our absence. All three of us wept for them that night, and we never saw the three crows again.

ONE ADVANTAGE that the country-bred boy has that the city-bred boy rarely enjoys is the affection and companionship of farm animals. We had innumerable pets and we loved them as they loved us. We had a dog and a cat and, at times, pups and kittens. We had pet lambs. We had our own horses, and a horse can be as affectionate as a dog. We had pet pigs, and no pet can be more interesting or better fun than a baby pig. We had our favorite cows and calves. We had a name for every animal on the farm, excepting the poultry, and a cow would be known, for instance, as "Bossy" or "Spotty," as if it were a person, and not a cow or a calf. Each of us boys had his quota of animals allotted to him and he took care of them as if they were his very own. This was doubtless a bit of smart scheming by Grandfather; but it brought difficulties, for we got to know a creature so well and to love it so much that we would fuss, and sometimes weep, when it had to be sold at the market or slaughtered for the table.

This recalls the time that Aunt Theresa, Grandfather's elderly maiden sister, hired us to kill her aged and decrepit tomcat, "William."

Aunt Theresa lived alone with "William" and a dog named "Silver" on a small farm adjoining Grandfather's. She was always kind to us and we were frequent visitors to her home; but our major interest in her and her farm was centered in her apple orchard, which was the best in Washabuckt. In the apple season we were daily, and uninvited, guests in her orchard, for our love of apples was far beyond the measure of her generosity. In our rush and greed it seems we sometimes broke limbs from the trees and did other damage besides ravaging the orchard's crop. Her protests got us whippings from Grandfather, which neither curbed our appetite for the apples nor our raids on the orchard.

So one day Aunt Theresa sent for us and made a proposition. She had decided reluctantly that "William" had come to the end of his days. If we would dispose of him humanely she would reward us with a basket of her choice apples. She figured the deal would cost her nothing; she would get rid of the old cat for apples that we would take anyway. We agreed, and departed with "William." His death, she stressed as we left, had to be sudden and painless.

The four of us, three boys and the cat, sat down on the grass in the shade of a huge beech tree on the bank of the nearby brook to think things over. We had had experience with drowning young and still blind kittens, but "William" was a different problem. The more we looked at him and the more he looked back at us the more difficult it became.

We quickly decided that drowning was out of the question, for we could not get him under water or hold him there. Little Murdoch suggested that as a cat had nine lives we might have to do it over nine times and should get a basket of apples for each. Big Murdoch thought it might be a good idea to make him a target for our bows and arrows, but that did not seem like a humane way of doing it. We discussed other forms of execution until I finally came up with the proposal to hang him from one of the limbs of the beech tree. This was agreeable to all of us, except "William," for we knew it was the way that the law dealt with men and so it must be the most humane of all deaths.

Then arose the problem of how to hang a cat. We decided to do it in the best hangman's way. We got several empty boxes from Aunt Theresa's barn and the rope reins from Grandfather's barn. We stacked the boxes one on the other under the beech tree and sat "William" on top of them. Then we made a noose of one end of the rope reins and threw the other end over the biggest outstretching limb of the tree. Finally we put the noose about "William's" neck and tightened it and, that done, suddenly kicked the boxes from under him.

We sat about in the grass waiting for "William" to die his humane death. "William," however, was in no hurry to depart this life. He wiggled about and swung back and forth and made faces at us as if to reproach us; and kept on living. In fact, he seemed to be enjoying the execution. This went on until he exhausted our patience, which was short, for we were eager to get the apples. So we left him dangling from the tree and returned to Aunt Theresa and reported him dead. We got the basket of apples; ate our fill of them; and went swimming in the Lake. We promptly forgot about "William."

Next day we dropped around casually to pay Aunt Theresa a visit, hoping to get some more apples. The first thing to face us on opening the door of her home was "William," still old and decrepit but none the worse for the hanging. We departed quickly and silently. To this day we cannot figure out how "William" did it.

That afternoon Grandfather's reins were discovered hanging from the beech tree and all three of us got a whipping for taking them. Thereupon we decided that virtue did not pay, for if we were to get whipped anyway it might just as well have been for stealing the apples. And it would have been easier for "William."

So our life on Grandfather's farm was merry and interesting and educational while it lasted, despite its hardships and inconveniences. But a boy does not remain a boy and all good things must end, for in the nature of things a boy becomes a man with a man's work and worry.

CHAPTER NINE

The Girl from Philadelphia

THE APPEARANCE OF The Girl from Philadelphia on the Washabuckt scene shook its society to its deepest roots. In truth it was never quite the same again.

Her first visit, like other events that have had profound influence on humanity, was unexpected, unheralded and perhaps fortuitous, although few things that The Girl from Philadelphia did were not done by design or without foreknowledge of the consequences. For her, life was indeed a stage on which she had a dramatic role to play, and she planned her entrances and her exits with the astute cunning of a Duse or a Bernhardt. Anyway there happened to be a picnic in Washabuckt to raise funds for the church that was being built and people from all over the parish came to help the good cause and to enjoy the fun. That was how and when she came.

She had been visiting her grandparents in Barra Glen, a modest farming settlement in the mountains back of Iona and about ten miles from Washabuckt. Her people had been among the pioneers and up to that time were unknown to fame. Her father, it seems, had left Cape Breton some twenty-odd years before and after some years in Boston had moved on to Philadelphia.

There he had prospered and married and was reported to be still occupied with the raising of a large family. The Girl from Philadelphia was his eldest child and the first of his family to return to the home of his ancestors.

She no doubt had a name as did her father and her grandfather before her, and no doubt a beautiful one, but if so I never heard of it, for she was known in Washabuckt only as The Girl from Philadelphia.

Neither was Philadelphia known, except as a vague and mysterious spot on the map where strange people lived in strange ways. Nobody from Washabuckt had ever strayed there, or at least if they did they did not return to tell about it. But Philadelphia was destined to become in Washabuckt the best-known city in the world, apart from Boston, and it was not long before the young gallants of the neighborhood were referring to it in such intimate terms as "Philly" and "The City of Brotherly Love."

The Girl from Philadelphia not only stole the show at the picnic, she became the whole show, for all the other attractions were neglected. Wherever she walked about the grounds crowds followed in her wake. When she stopped they gathered about to look and listen. As she swished through the lancers on the dancing platform scores closed in to gape and wonder. She pretended to be unconscious of the commotion she was causing. At least she gave no outward indication of anything unusual. Perhaps she was accustomed to such admiration and adulation.

Hitherto the Washabuckters had not been aware that such creatures walked the earth. Of course they had seen pictures of modish ladies in the latest styles in the fashion magazines that occasionally reached the community; but they did not believe that these were pictures of real persons. They felt that such visions existed only in the imagination of the artist, like William Blake's illustration of the ghost of a flea. Yet here they were seeing one of these wonderful creatures tripping lightly and gaily about the picnic grounds. They could scarcely credit their eyes. The reappearance of Cleopatra could not have stirred them more deeply.

The Girl from Philadelphia was everything that the Washabuckt girls were not. Where they were simple, she was artificial. They were modest and retiring; she was daring and forward. They strove to conceal their femininity; she flaunted hers. The contrast was startling. Favored by nature to begin with, she employed every art and wile to improve her beauty and allure. She was the painted lily in a field of daisies.

She had a mass of blond hair that had known peroxide and was done up in a high pompadour with golden curls dropping about in the most unexpected places. Her eyebrows were tinted a jet black and plucked and arched in a way that would have amazed her Creator. Her blue eyes sparkled with the brilliance of belladonna. Her lips were rouged into cupid bows. Her cheeks and neck were powdered like the bloom of a peach with spots of color in the right places to give them piquancy and drama. Her fingernails, the longest Washabuckt had ever seen, were filed to sharp points and shellacked and polished until they glistened in the summer sun. Overall she was saturated with a perfume that pervaded the entire picnic grounds.

Her dress was beyond masculine description with its ribbons, frills, pleats and yards of silk that reached the floor; but even a boy could notice that it was something interesting and extraordinary. Of course, it was in the very latest mode, and fitted and draped to make the most of her sylph-like figure, slender and supple with the right bulges and the right curves in the right places and in the right proportions. It seemed that the mode was made for her and she for the mode, so well did one blend into the other. But her petticoats were the sensation of the day.

Naturally, I do not know how many there were, but they were made of taffeta that hummed and rustled at every movement. As she was never still and would swish her skirts and petticoats about her with long, slow sweeps she gave a performance that was a wonder to behold and she made a music of her own that was pleasant to hear, and set Washabuckt manhood ablaze.

Every movement she made was studied to stress her elegant and fluid figure or some other feminine charm or challenge. When she sat, she did so with a slough and crossed her legs in a manner to show a tiny foot encased in a high-heeled French slipper and about six inches of a well-turned and silk-clad ankle. Washabuckt women in those days were not supposed to have legs, or at least no one was supposed to see them. And when she walked she found occasion to gather her skirts and petticoats about her coyly and gracefully and thus give furtive glimpses of her slippers and ankles.

Her conversation was equally extraordinary to Washabuckt. It had accents, intonations, modulations and she made gestures that had not been heard or seen before. It contained references and allusions that had no local meaning and was interspersed with slang words and idioms that were new to local ears. Besides, it was a mixture of timidity and audacity that at once charmed and shocked her Washabuckt listeners.

Whether she had the greater impact on the men or the women, it is impossible to tell, for each sex was hit hard, but in different ways. Women, old and young, buzzed about her in wide-eyed amazement and picked her to pieces as they appraised and commented on her dress, her make-up, her posture, her talk, with not one item escaping their curiosity and wonder. Men, young and old, fluttered about her like moths about a candle, afraid that they would be burned and fearful that they would not.

Old Betsy probably said the last word for feminine

Washabuckt when she called her a "pagan." Ronald son of Dan Angus doubtless said the last word for the male sex when he gasped: "Boy! Oh, Boy!"

One thing was certain and that was that both sexes in Washabuckt had not seen enough of The Girl from Philadelphia.

So the church picnic was the beginning of a lively social season. The girls got their parents to give dances and the young men found some excuse for parties. The Girl from Philadelphia was always invited and she always came, no matter the distance or the weather. And she always appeared in a new hair-do and yet another gown. Neither her endurance nor her capacity for enjoyment seemed to have a limit. The more parties the more merry and more vivacious she became. She radiated her charm and wiles on all present without stint or discrimination. She was willing at all times to talk over a girl's problems with the girls and to make small talk to the men. But she avoided close intimacy with any member of either sex.

Young gallants who thought they were in love with her, but more likely were merely dazzled by her presence, she put gently but firmly in their places; and each was grateful afterwards, for no one was such a fool as to think that she could be maintained on a Washabuckt farm on a Washabuckt income. Some threatened to follow her to "Philly," where they could make good in a big American way and be near her, but these she did not encourage either. So they had to make the most of her while they had her and to accept what of her time and pleasure she could give them then and there. There was nothing else to be done about it.

These young bloods, naturally shy and awkward, found making talk with her a bit difficult until they hit upon the idea of initiating her into Cape Breton ways of doing things. Here they discovered her greatest immediate interest. She wanted to know all about life on a farm. In return she told them all about life in Philadelphia and how things were done there. She was ready to give as well as take. So it was that she agreed to teach them how to play baseball if they would teach her how to milk a cow.

Within a week she was ready to give them the first lesson in baseball. Most of the young men for miles around gathered that afternoon in the pasture of her grandfather's farm, where she had laid out a baseball diamond. For the occasion she had made a ball of twine and she had her grandfather make several bats from birch timber. She could not get gloves and a mask, but she later explained that the soft ball made these unnecessary. She made up two rival teams from among the boys.

First she explained the basic rules of the game and its purposes. Then she demonstrated how to pitch, how to catch, how to bat and how to run bases. This done, she appointed herself umpire and ordered the game to start. But the game just could not start, for all the boys were more intent on gaping at her or rushing to do her some feigned service than in doing what she had asked them to do. However, it was all very gay and amusing and The Girl from Philadelphia laughed until the tears came to her eyes and threatened to mar her make-up. Thereupon she ended the lesson and served the boys a picnic on the grass. This was better, for they could eat and still gape at her.

The lesson in milking was much of a kind, pleasant but futile. A troop of her admirers led her to a cow pasture, where a cow named "Spot" had been chosen for the demonstration. One gallant carried the pail, another the stool, and the rest of them came in her train. Marie Antoinette did not have more courtiers in the days when she, too, tried her hand at milking, nor did she approach the task more regally.

The pail was placed under the cow. The stool was

fixed on the right side, although one wag tried to put it on the left. The Girl from Philadelphia gathered her voluminous skirts and petticoats about her and sat herself on the stool in one of her most entrancing poses. One of the boys called attention to the swollen udder and the four protruding fat teats. Another showed her how to spit in her hands, for this was the Washabuckt way of moistening and lubricating both the hands and the teats, and the first preliminary to all milking operations.

Then and only then it was discovered that she was wearing flesh-coloured gloves on her dainty hands.

"Oh, dear!" she exclaimed. "That is simply impossible!"

At that instant "Spot" decided to swing her tail and it caught The Girl from Philadelphia right across the face in the most disconcerting manner.

The instructors kept insisting that it was necessary to spit in her hands and she kept insisting that that was one thing she could not and would not do. Finally "Spot" decided that something had to be done about it; so she walked off. On the first step she planted her big, mud-covered hoof in the pail, and swishing her tail knocked The Girl off the stool.

The Girl from Philadelphia took it all in good part, and again laughed merrily and long at all the fun they were having. Later the farmer's wife milked "Spot" along with the other cows.

The doings and the sayings of The Girl from Philadelphia supplied Washabuckt with gossip for weeks. There seemed to be no end of it. When she did not do something peculiar she said something that astounded everybody. Her clothes, her make-up, each hair-do kept the women and the girls talking eternally, sometimes in whispers. They had spies who even entered her room. All kinds of reports made the rounds, some of them doubtless exaggerated. Word got about, for instance, that she had six trunks full of clothes, and one trunk full of mysterious boxes, bottles and instruments for her make-up. But what really set the neighborhood on its ear was the report that she was by occupation a manicure.

There was much speculation as to what a manicure really was, for the word as well as the vocation was unknown to Washabuckt. Some one asked Crooked Dan about it and he hazarded the guess that it was a form of nursing, probably a nurse for men. Others doubted that there was such an occupation. One youth insisted that she had spelled out the word and that there could be no doubt about it. Finally some one suggested that they should look up the word in a dictionary.

So a party of boys and girls came to Grandfather's home one night to consult his dictionary. What they found in the dictionary they could scarcely believe, although it had been written by Mr. Webster himself. They found that the word "manicure" came from two Latin words, "manus," meaning "hand," and "cura," meaning "care," and that the word meant a person whose job was to care for hands and trim nails.

Such a way of making a living had never been considered in their wildest dreams. Only The Girl from Philadelphia could think of such a thing. In Washabuckt, if a lady, you cut your nails with a pair of scissors; if a man, with a jack-knife; and why any one should have to go to a "manicure" they could not figure out.

As this seemed the ultimate in indolence and luxury they concluded that the clients of a "manicure" must be those ladies of fashion and wealth with nothing to do and too much money to spend. They asked The Girl from Philadelphia about it and got another severe shock. She announced blithely in the presence of a dozen persons that she did not serve women but men. She worked, she explained, in a barbershop and trimmed nails while the men were getting a haircut or a shave.

The Washabuckt estimate of the manhood of Philadelphia took a sharp drop. Some one asked if they wore
skirts. Another suggested that this might be the reason
Philadelphia was known as the City of Brotherly Love.
And one wag regaled the neighborhood with laughter by
going up to every girl he met and asking her to cut his
nails. The whole thing seemed fantastic, incredible.

Some of the boys and the girls wanted to question
The Girl from Philadelphia further on the matter, but before they got the chance she packed her trunks and left.

Washabuckt never heard of her again; and after some
months began slowly to recover its calm.

CHAPTER TEN

Washabuckt's Own Millionaire

STRANGE THINGS HAPPEN in all large families and in all communities, things for which there may be no easy explanation, scientific or spiritual, like a dwarf in a family of giants, an albino Negro, a poet in a hovel, or a double-headed calf. Many strange things happened in Washabuckt too, and the most extraordinary of them was the fact that one of its native sons turned out to be a millionaire, a genuine, authenticated millionaire, a cross between Midas and Crœsus.

Of all places in the world, apart perhaps from the jungles of Africa, Washabuckt would be one of the last that would be expected to produce such a man. The Washabuckt native did not think in terms of money for he was seldom conscious of the need of cash, got along very well with little of it, and had other standards. He was not a money-grabber. The head of a family was considered well-to-do if he could hand over a five-dollar bill when there was desperate want of it. Land could be bought for as little as one dollar an acre. Farm labor was content to work for fifty cents a day and board—an eleven- or twelve-hour day, or from dawn to dusk. Rarely did the Washabuckter have as much as one hundred dollars at one time, and such an occasion would certainly be after the sale of property or a bountiful crop and some livestock.

Moreover, the Gaelic-speaking Washabuckter of those days, before two World Wars upset the economic reasoning of most peoples and popularized thinking in billions, had no way of expressing himself in terms of millions. The largest figure that I had heard mentioned in Washabuckt Gaelic was 100,000 and that was in the salutation "ceud mìle fàilte," literally "100,000 greetings," a figure that was felt to approach infinity in a greeting that was considered the ultimate in welcomes. The Washabuckter had no more conception of what a million meant in dollars than he had of what it meant in light-years. To him it was simply something fabulous, an accumulation of dollars that could not be spent in a lifetime of luxurious living, which in turn meant good food, good clothes, a good home, and an unlimited supply of tobacco and whiskey.

Of course the Millionaire did not accumulate his money in Washabuckt. All the cash that had reached Washabuckt from its first settlement and all that will ever reach it before Judgment Day and oblivion would not total up to a million dollars. Like other natives, the Millionaire had gone to the Boston States in his youth and there he and his three brothers had been successful in the building business. There was always some mystery about how he got so much money while his partner-brothers remained men of moderate means, and some unpleasant reports reached Washabuckt about it. We shall not go into such things here except to remark that most millionaires are made that way, and ours was no exception.

In Washabuckt the Millionaire was a compound of fiction and fact and at once a legend and a reality. Stories about him and his wealth, one more fantastic than the other, circulated the neighborhood, all doubtless with a basis in fact but grossly exaggerated. Then when he would begin to assume the proportions of a figure in the Arabian Nights he would visit Washabuckt in person, and move about among his relatives and old friends, like a Hollywood movie star exposing himself to his public, and with much the same results.

One story was told about his audacity. As a young, inexperienced man he got a job as a carpenter. He was set to work making window-frames. After a time his employer came around to see how he was making out. The frame he was making was pretty much of a mess.

"That's the worst window-frame I have ever seen," remarked the Boss.

"There are worse ones," retorted the future Millionaire.

"Is that so!" demanded the Boss. "Where could you find a worse one?"

"Here," replied the Washabuckt youth, pulling out one of his earlier efforts from under his bench.

Another story was told of his loyalty to his Scottish ancestry. Some years later when he was a prominent Boston contractor and already a millionaire, he visited one of the buildings he had under construction. As he entered the structure he noticed a mechanic hanging a pair of double doors. He stopped for some minutes to admire the mechanic's efficiency and artistry, for this is one of the most exacting tasks in carpentry. He then proceeded through the building for his inspection. Leaving about an hour later, he stopped again to watch the mechanic at work. Evidently intending either to promote him or give him a raise in pay, he asked his name.

"My name is Menteith," responded the man.

The Millionaire was shocked.

"Are you related to the man who betrayed William Wallace?" he inquired.

"Oh, I suppose so," replied the mechanic, "but that was nearly 600 years ago."

"That makes no difference," retorted the Millionaire. "I don't employ traitors. Get off the job."

And he discharged him on the spot.

Further evidence of his loyalty to his Scottish ancestry is the fact that he was the first of the family to return on a visit to Barra. He did so in style. He chartered a yacht in Glasgow, loaded it with casks of whiskey, and headed for the island home of his fathers, certain of a cordial welcome. The yacht dropped anchor in Castlebay, but before the Millionaire put in an appearance he ordered numerous casks of the liquor to be placed on the dock. With each cask was a large tin dipper. That done, the heads of the casks were stove in; and the populace was invited to come and drink its fill.

That day will probably be remembered in Barra as long as will be the landing of Bonnie Prince Charlie on the soil of the MacNeils.

Many decades later an old seaman came up to speak to me on the deck of one of the Atlantic liners. He was a Barraman; and somehow he had learned of my kinship with the Millionaire. As a young man he had drunk some of that whiskey. He still spoke of the occasion with reverance and awe.

All the Cape Breton boys, and especially the Washabuckt boys, who headed for the United States were certain of work with the Millionaire. Dozens of them were always employed on his projects, mostly at common labor and always at long hours and low wages. This circumstance added to his fame. Many of these men returned to their homes with stories of his personal splendor, of his great homes, his horses and carriages, and his many doingså with the other great people of Boston. They also told far and wide of the tremendous buildings he built or was building throughout the New England States. Later some returned with reports that the work was harder and the pay lower and the hours longer than with other employers. There were also reports of sharp practices. Generally these reports were ignored in the fabulous glamour.

Before my appearance on the Washabuckt scene the Millionaire had built himself an "elegant" summer palace at Baddeck with striking views of the Lake and the beautiful bordering countryside. Nearby he had also built homes for some favorite relatives. All these homes were in the gaudy architecture and pretentious bad taste of the 1880's and 1890's. Here on occasion the Millionaire held court with much of the pomposity of the Medici but without their devotion to the arts.

About his golden splendor, fluttered a score or so of admiring sisters, nieces and nephews. They were the Millionaire's palace guard. In residence they buzzed about him like the drones about the queen bee in the hive, and when he ventured out he had more satellites swirling about him than Jupiter has moons. With no income taxes and the populace still impressed by the power of the dollar, life was pleasant for a man of wealth at the turn of the century.

All kinds of reports reached Washabuckt. There were reports of Lucullan feasts and many other extravagances. There were also reports of all manner of intrigue—intrigue to win favor for the self-designated guardian angels and intrigue to stop or block the selfish machinations of alien intruders. In fact, there were those who intimated that the House of the Borgias had nothing on the House of the Millionaire. One thing is certain— that the millionaire provided all that money could buy, and that was not a little; and life was interesting and colorful.

Great as was the stir that the Millionaire made in Baddeck society it was as nothing compared with the commotion his visits caused in his native Washabuckt. He kept these visits rare for they were too good to spoil. He enjoyed them to the full. Washabuckt enjoyed them also; and was always ready to be thrilled once again. Moreover, each visit was good for months of gossip afterwards.

These were the Millionaire's personal triumphs and he came to Washabuckt with much of the dignity and pomp of the conquering general returning to Rome from the wars on the barbarians. He always came with a retinue of admiring relatives. The well-tailored clothes of fine materials that covered his expansive girth were noted and commented on. So also were the other evidences of wealth, the big gold watch and its chain, the rings with huge precious stones, and the fat roll of bills. Neither did Washabuckt miss the casual remarks about friends among the great of the United States and about the doing of great things. The poor Washabuckt relatives were nearly always overwhelmed into silence, even when they profited financially, but if they did not say much they missed nothing. So far as is known not one of them asked:

"Upon what meat doth this our Caesar feed
That he is grown so great?"

ONE PERSON IN WASHABUCKT was not unduly impressed, and that was Grandfather.

While I was at Grandfather's home word came one day that the Millionaire had landed in Washabuckt with the usual bevy of relatives and was headed our way. Reports of his progress through the community kept reaching Grandfather's home. Word came that he had given five dollars to this old lady, and five dollars to that old couple, and so on. It was always five dollars, and peeled ostentatiously off the roll of paper money. This was, of course, before the time John D. Rockefeller started distributing his largesse in dimes; and then five dollars was a lot of money in Washabuckt.

It would buy a barrel of flour, and a barrel of flour would allow a needy family to survive for two months.

Finally he and his retinue arrived in a fleet of carriages and two bicycles. They were met by Grandfather with a warm welcome and escorted into the seldom-used parlor.

My recollection of the Millionaire is of a huge man with a prominent paunch emphasized by the gold watch-chain that stretched across it; a heavy-set, serious face with jowls and a large, drooping moustache; two thick, fat but strong, hands; thick ankles and large feet; and a booming, blustering voice.

He sat down in the place of honor without being invited to do so and the members of his party made themselves as comfortable as they could in the small room. Grandfather undertook conversation with the great man, while Grandmother rushed to the kitchen to prepare tea.

The talk had not gone far before Grandfather remarked:

"You are a very rich man."

"Well, I have a bit of money, enough to get along on."

"Does it bother you much?"

"What do you mean by 'bother'? I find it rather handy at times."

This retort brought a snicker from some of the relatives.

"Does it trouble your conscience?"

"No, why should it?"

"Don't you know what Christ said about the rich man getting into Heaven?"

"Well, yes, I do; but what has that got to do with me?"

"Let me remind you of what Christ Himself said."

With that Grandfather picked up his Gaelic Bible,

which he had obviously placed near at hand, and started to read the nineteenth chapter of Matthew in a voice that sounded like the voice of doom. There was an uneasy stirring about the room. Some of those present understood the rolling Gaelic sentences, others did not. No one felt comfortable. When Grandfather finished the 26th verse he closed the book, and placed it on the table.

"I am afraid my Gaelic is not so good," the Millionaire started to explain.

"Well, then, let me read it to you in English," insisted Grandfather. "I'm sure you will want to know every word of it. It is most important for you."

He left the room for a minute and returned with a copy of the Douay translation of the Bible, sat down again with dignity, looked about the room in silence for a long time, and then said:

"A young man, a very rich young man, asked Christ what he should do to be saved. What Christ said to him and his talk later with the Apostles about it is told by St. Matthew in these words:

21. Jesus saith to him: If thou wilt be perfect, go sell what thou hast and give to the poor, and thou shalt have treasure in Heaven: and come, follow Me.

22. And when the young man had heard this word, he went away sad: for he had great possessions.

23. Then Jesus said to his disciples: Amen I say to you, that a rich man shall hardly enter into the kingdom of heaven.

24. And again I say to you: It is easier for the camel to pass through the eye of a needle than for a rich man to enter the kingdom of heaven.

25. And when they had heard this, the disciples wondered very much, saying: Who then shall be saved?

26. And Jesus beholding, said to them: With men this is impossible: but with God all things are possible."

On ending the reading, Grandfather reached over and

placed the Bible on the table with firm deliberation, looked about the room again in silence, and awaited an answer. It was an awkward moment. The relatives sat gazing at the Millionaire and the Millionaire sat gazing at the floor. At last he spoke.

"That is not as bad as it sounds. If you make your money honestly...."

"Christ did not say anything about honesty. He said a 'rich' man; any rich will do."

"But you cannot be damned for making money honestly."

"Christ seems to think you can. He ought to know what He is talking about. These are His exact words."

"Quite right, but He did not mean the eye of an ordinary needle. He was using a figure of speech. In His time there was a hole, or entrance, in the walls of the City of Jerusalem called 'The Eye of the Needle.' That is what He meant. A camel could get through it standing if it were a small camel, or by stooping if it were a large camel."

"The Bible is clear, very clear. It says 'a' needle, not 'the' needle. That means any needle, the needle a woman uses to sew a shirt, or a petticoat."

Here Grandmother entered the room with dishes for the serving of the tea.

"Mother, bring me a needle," Grandfather ordered.

Grandmother found her sewing-basket and handed him a needle. Grandfather held it up to the light of the window so he could the better see it.

"This is a darning needle," he said. "It is too big. Bring me an ordinary needle, a sewing needle."

She got him a tiny needle from the basket. He handled it gingerly, for he had difficulty in seeing it. He held it up to the light, but you could not see its eye. He put on his spectacles, and looked again, and at last satisfied himself.

"There you are," he said. "This is the kind of needle

that is mentioned in the Bible. This is what Christ meant. You cannot get away from it. A camel would certainly have a job getting through its eye. A camel is bigger than a horse."

With that he walked across the room and held up the needle in front of the Millionaire, remarking as he did so:

"A camel is bigger than a horse or a cow."

It was an impressive demonstration, and watching it, I began to feel sorry for the Millionaire and all other rich men. For if their chances of getting into heaven were no better than those of a camel, or a horse, or a cow, getting through the eye of that needle, their chances were slim indeed. The Milliionaire's case looked hopeless.

At that point Grandmother started to serve the tea. Grandfather, having proved what he set out to prove, let the matter drop. The conversation returned to the usual banalities. And soon after drinking his cup of tea, the Millionaire made his excuses, and left with his retainers; a bit crestfallen, I thought.

What effect Grandfather's reading of Matthew and of his demonstration with the needle had on the Millionaire I have no way of knowing, never having been in his confidence. I do know this, however, for it is common knowledge, that a few years later he became deeply interested in religion and abnormally generous to the Church. He made large gifts for churches, rectories, church schools, and charities. When he died his fortune was but a fraction of what it had been, and that also he left to the Church.

CHAPTER ELEVEN

Black Dan, the Clockmaker

BLACK DAN WAS VERSATILE or nothing. He could do most anything he tried to do. He farmed, fished, trapped, cobbled, tailored, wrote satirical Gaelic songs, sang them, played the bagpipes and gossiped; but above all he was noted as the neighborhood Clockmaker. With his spinster sister and bachelor brother, he, himself also a bachelor, lived in a small frame cabin on a few cleared acres beside a tumbling brook in a remote glen in the mountain forests, far from the next neighbor. Yet he missed few social functions for miles in all directions, for he loved parties and he was the life of every one he attended with his storytelling, his Gaelic songs, his piping and his boisterous spirit of fun.

Once a year Black Dan took to the road as a clockmaker, his pipes in a wooden box in one hand and his satchel of tools in the other. He was popular everywhere he went, for it usually meant another frolic. In a month or six weeks he made his grand tour of the neighboring communities. He usually reached Grandfather's home just before the spring planting and stayed overnight with us.

Grandfather always had a hearty welcome for Black Dan. They were old cronies. No matter what Grandfather had been doing before his arrival he stopped it, and spent the rest of the day and the night with Black Dan. Nor would he let Black Dan do any work that day; that, he said, could be done the next morning. The old man wanted to talk to Black Dan, to hear his latest songs, and, of course, to have him play the pipes.

The Clockmaker came well equipped to entertain. As he moved from house to house, and neighborhood to neighborhood, he collected all the available gossip and this he would tell with relish. He was the antecedent of the modern journalistic keyhole watchers. While he talked the women would sit around and listen, or if they had some household task they still kept within hearing distance, and Grandfather for once would not interrupt a speaker.

Black Dan's news would be recounted in a dramatic voice, interspersed with moral precepts, and would run something like this:

"Red Malcolm the Long One has not been able to pay the county taxes. They are going to sell his farm from the steps of the county court in Baddeck. Too much whiskey! Little Rory's wife is going to have another baby. The eleventh. Another mouth to feed. Rory must do some more scratching. Ronald the Pepper got drunk at Baddeck. He thrashed his wife and five of the children, one after the other. His wife went to the Priest. He made Ronald take the pledge. Serves him right. Mrs. Allen Peter the Framer got a letter from her daughter in Boston. There was five dollars in it. She sent it to Eaton's in Toronto to buy Allen a new Sunday suit. He will be a sight to see! Hector Little Hector and his family are living on potatoes and salt. He never did have any gumption. No more credit at the stores. He's too lazy to fish or hunt. I fixed their clock for nothing. Dan the Banker's son has three calves and eight lambs already. The Devil is good to his own. Jane the Brook has dropsy. She's a mess. She spends all her time saying her beads. It's time she gave a thought to the next world."

And so the Clockmaker would rattle on for an hour or more until he had covered all his gossip. He was better than a local newspaper with one annual edition, for he missed nothing, no matter how trivial. Everybody liked to listen to his chitchat, but everybody knew that he himself or his family might well be part of his story at his next stop. No one minded much, for each one was so eager to hear about his neighbor that he would risk what might be said of himself, and then the gossip was never malicious. The same, however, could not be said for his Gaelic songs.

"Any new songs, Dan?" Grandfather would inquire after a time.

"Oh, I have no time for songs any more," the Clockmaker would reply. "But I did get up one about Raggedy Ann and Flora the Rat. They met in battle on the Road to Iona. They were on their way to Mass on Sunday morning. That made no difference. They fought it out while the boys cheered them on. They tore hair and clothes. After it was over what was left of them went home. They did not have enough clothes left to go to Mass. But it was a glorious fight!"

Thereupon he would put down his cup of tea, and in a loud but musical voice he would launch into his newest song. It was always a mixture of satire, humor and narrative, with a bite or a laugh in every phrase. His songs more often than not dealt with a fight of some kind, although they might deal with any human passion or activity. I remember that one dealt with the misfortune of Tight Hugh, the miser, who gave the priest fifty cents, when he had intended, with much reluctance, to give him twenty-five cents. Still another did ample justice to Fancy Mike the Carpenter, who thought that all the Washabuckt girls were in love with him when in reality they were having some fun at his expense.

While everybody, and especially Grandfather, liked to hear Black Dan sing his own songs, no one wanted to be the hero or heroine of one of his efforts. That brought a quick, local notoriety and a promise of immortality that no one seemed to desire. Fortunately, or perhaps unfortunately, Black Dan could not write in Gaelic, and not so well in English, so he never put his songs or translations of them on to paper. There were people who did memorize some of them, but they did not dare try to sing them, for they could not do justice to them. They simply could not put the proper bite and humor into them. The Clockmaker was an actor who made up his own lines. So most of Black Dan's songs did not last long, and all disappeared from the scene of his triumphs when what was mortal of the master went the way of all flesh.

The Clockmaker's forte, however, was the playing of the bagpipes. Here he was the artist supreme, temperamental and competent. Grandfather maintained that he was the best piper in Cape Breton, bar none. Black Dan himself would not deny it, and there were few who would dispute it, certainly not in Washabuckt.

On each visit Black Dan would give a special, private concert just for Grandfather. The two of them would retire to the parlor. Black Dan would take the pipes from their box with an air of reverence, and adjust them. Grandfather would compliment him on their fine quality and note their silk streamers of MacNeil tartan. With much blowing, Black Dan would fill the bag with air, do some nimble fingering on the chanter to limber his fingers, tune the three drones one to the other and all three to the chanter, and after these rites indicate that he was ready and at Grandfather's service. The Old Man always called the tunes, and he invariably started with "Callum Gille," which, incidentally, is the tune for the Sword Dance. In his younger days, Grandfather would leap to the floor and do the intricate and stirring steps. Next he would call for "The Cock of the North," and the concert would be under way.

Apart from the music it was a sight worth seeing, and we boys usually contrived to see it, peeking through one of the windows. Black Dan would sit straight on a hard chair, his fingers flying over the chanter, his face blue from the strain and puffed out to the size of a pumpkin as he fed breath to the bag, and his feet, sometimes one foot and sometimes two, keeping time for the music. Meanwhile Grandfather would sit back in an easy chair, slowly smoking his pipe, and in a semitrance of delight. In succession and at Grandfather's call, Black Dan would produce reels, marches, strathspeys, and the concert usually ended with "MacCrimmon's Lament," its slow, sad melodies, the most woeful and weird sounds ever heard on earth.

There are those, and they are many, who scoff at the music of the bagpipes, and many even contend that it is not music at all. Sad indeed is their lot, for they cannot appreciate one of the most ennobling and thrilling experiences of life. They forget or never knew that the pibroch was the first music of all the peoples of the Western world and started them upward on the rise from savagery.

The bagpipes were introduced into the British Isles by Roman soldiers, and it was from the Legions that the Scots and the Irish got them. Their music has an elemental quality, like the music of the spheres that the poets dream about, that lifts the soul and quickens the body. Who would deny the brave deeds that the bagpipes have inspired on innumerable battlefields and the victories they have wrought? They encouraged Bruce at Bannockburn; sounded the doom of Napoleon at Waterloo; led Montgomery's advance over the sands of El Alamein and thus marked the beginning of the end of Hitler and his Nazi hordes. Perhaps the pibroch demands a simple mysticism that the hardheaded and soulless pragmatists of today cannot muster. Like the shrill, sweet song of the bird, it is the music of nature. Possibly that is why it is enjoyed most and cherished by the whimsical and mystical Celts of Southern Ireland and of the Highlands and Islands of Scotland.

The music of the bagpipes, like every other kind of music, cannot be understood or appreciated unless it is heard in its proper and natural setting. It is not the music of the music hall, although it has been played there, and when you confine it within walls and a ceiling it is like chaining the lion to a tree or caging an eagle. The pibroch is the music of the glens and the lakes, of the woods and the mountains, of the campfire and the dark night, of the marching men and the battlefield. It is heroic music. It can also be bright or sad, the music of the stirring dance and the dirge for the fallen hero. It is a soulful music for soulful people.

I heard the pibroch once as it should be heard. One summer evening found me strolling leisurely along a wooded road that skirted the Lake. The sun had set in vivid splendor about a half hour before and the heavy darkness of night was beginning to settle over the Washabuckt landscape. The stress and turmoil of the day had ended for me, and I was reveling in that spiritual hour that is neither day nor night when a boy feels at peace with himself and the world. Through the trees I could catch glimpses of the calm waters of the Lake and of the purple and maroon skies above. Occasionally a furtive bird would fly with a noisy swish across the road, on its way home to its nest for the night. A thousand frogs were singing their twilight lullabies. Here and there a fish would leap in the waters with a loud splash.

Suddenly I hard the oars of a boat rowing several hundred yards off the shore. It came as a shock, for I had been unconscious of anything but nature and eternity. The rhythmic swing of the oars in the oarlocks and in the water made a music that was not unpleasant and did not disturb the scene. Through an opening in the trees I saw a boat with two figures in it, one at the oars and one sitting in the stern. As I stood watching and listening and wondering what it was all about and who were in the boat, the shrill notes of the bagpipes came across the waters. The figure in the stern was a piper and he was tuning his instrument. That done, he played "The Flowers of the Forest."

The music floated through the twilight over the water and through the trees and echoed from hill to hill until it enveloped the scene. It could have been Pan himself, playing a tune before retiring for the night. The harsher notes were mellowed by the sounding board of nature and the melody danced gaily over the land. All the polyphonic rhythms blended and harmonized with the sounds of nature and became part of the noble scene until one felt that God and his angels and all the myriad creatures He had made were listening too, and happy to do so. It was sublime music in a sublime setting, such music as is not often given to man to hear, but which one hopes may be one of the pleasures of Heaven. Here was the pibroch in its own setting as it had been known in the glens and by the lochs of Scotland.

In an ecstasy of delight I walked along the road keeping pace with the boat on the Lake so long as the music continued; and afterwards I stumbled home in the dark, exalted by the experience and too touched to speak of it.

A thousand times since I have heard what cosmopolites call great music. I have heard the music of the great composers interpreted by the greatest of artists of our day and by good fortune some of the latter have been my personal friends. I have been a subscriber to the Metropolitan Opera, Town Hall and Carnegie Hall in New

York. I have patronized the Royal Opera at Covent Garden and Albert Hall in London. I have attended the Opéra and the Opéra Comique in Paris. I have heard the operas of Wagner and Mozart sung in Germany and those of Verdi and Donizetti sung in Italy. I have heard the music of China, of Japan, of India, of Java. I have listened to soft serenades in Spain, to the tango in Latin America, to the rumba in Cuba. I know American jazz and jive. I admire the Negro spirituals. But never, anywhere, any time, have I heard music comparable in its sweetness and melody, in its majesty and sublimity, to the pibroch of that humble, unknown piper in a tub of a boat on the Bras d'Or Lakes on that summer's night.

THE CLOCKMAKER'S NIGHT at Grandfather's home meant a frolic. One by one and in groups the neighbors would come visiting. There was no invitation, for none was needed. All the younger folk for miles about would slip coyly and almost silently into the house and sit in corners. When the capacity of the kitchen was reaching its limit, Grandfather would suggest to Black Dan that he "play a tune or two on the pipes." Dan was always willing to oblige; and the fun was on.

Black Dan would begin with a march or two, something like "Highland Laddie," but he would soon turn to dance music. Some one would slyly suggest dancing, and Grandmother would suggest moving to the parlor, and the frolic would be under way. On occasion a fiddler also would mysteriously appear with his fiddle and bow, and the dancing would go on until the early morning. Sometimes there would be keen competition between the piper and the fiddler for favor, but it was difficult to beat Black Dan at his own game, and few did so. The piper would play for the Highland reels and the fiddler for the square dances, generally the lancers.

Grandfather always enjoyed the Highland Reel, and

when he was a young man made a reputation at it that survived until my day. I saw him dance it to pipe music at his golden wedding. He and Grandmother and the best man and bridesmaid, all four spry and gay after fifty years, stepped it out on the parlor floor. Grandfather had such fun and felt so good that he insisted on personally giving a drink to the piper. He disappeared into the dining room and returned with a goblet of liquor. The piper made a wry face and tried not to drink it, but Grandfather, thinking he was only pretending, made him drink the last drop of it. Unfortunately Grandfather had mistaken a bottle of red vinegar for the bottle of whiskey, and he nearly finished the piper. But pipers are tough, and this one lived out his days. It was the last time Grandfather danced himself, but he liked to watch others dance, especially if they were "fancy steppers."

It took wind and stamina to dance the Highland Reel as it was done in Washabuckt. Two rival couples took to the floor, each man facing his lady. All four stepdanced at a merry pace to the fast tempo of the music. After some minutes each man would swing his lady partner and then they would change partners in one wild but graceful swing. Then there would be more stepdancing and some more swinging and some more changing of partners until the music ended. Each gallant and each lady took pride in displaying a variety of steps, some of them extremely complex, and some of them of their own invention. Meanwhile the other guests would stand or sit about and cheer them on, clapping their hands in rhythm to the music, and often taunting the dancers. As the reel progressed the piper would speed up the tempo and the dancers would quicken their steps and the swings would become more vigorous and the applause more boisterous, until the four dancers were on the verge of collapse. It was grand fun; fun to dance, fun to watch.

The Clockmaker's visit would come to an end the

next morning, after he had done what he had come to do—to service Grandfather's clock. This was done whether it was needed or not. It was done yearly because it provided an excuse for Black Dan's visit.

Anyway Grandfather took pride in his clock and thought nothing was too good for it. It was a gift from my Father, who deliberately neglected to tell his father that it was an eight-day clock. Grandfather made a ritual of winding the clock every night, much to Father's amusement, and it was the signal for the household to retire for the night. When Grandfather stood up in all his dignity and reached for the key to the clock, we boys started for the outdoors regardless of the weather, as a necessary preparation for a long night's sleep.

Grandfather always took the clock down from the wall himself and placed it on the kitchen table, which Grandmother had meanwhile cleared for Black Dan's operations. There the Piper would proceed to disinter its guts, and he would soon have wheels and springs all over the table, and the poor clock would look like an empty and abandoned fruit crate. Looking from a safe distance we boys would wonder if he could get it back together again, but he always did. He would wipe parts of the clock and oil others and reassemble the whole machine with the greatest of ease while keeping up a line of chatter, which was partly technical to impress Grandmother and partly small gossip that he had forgotten about the day before. At last the clock would be placed back on the wall again, and would proceed to tick-tock for another year.

The job done, Grandfather would give the Clockmaker fifty cents, and with his bagpipes and kit of tools he would make his departure and after some minutes disappear up the road.

When he was well out of sight, Grandmother would take the broom and sweep the kitchen.

The last time I was present she swept up two tiny wheels and a delicate spring. She picked them up and looked at them and then looked wonderingly at the clock. It was tick-tocking nonchalantly and seemed none the worse for its experience and the loss of some of its intestines. Perhaps they were unnecessary organs like an appendix or tonsils.

We boys accepted this as the ultimate in clockmaking, for only a real clockmaker could make Grandfather's clock do its job with fewer wheels and springs than it had hitherto found necessary.

CHAPTER TWELVE

A Storm in Petticoats

BIG BETSY WAS IN HER LATE EIGHTIES when I knew her first and just skin and bones and a few straggling wisps of faded gray hair. Much of the flame and passion had left her aged body, but she was none the less the most turbulent spirit in Washabuckt. Her steel-blue eyes could still flash fire, and her tongue had lost little of its potency. Her command of Gaelic profanity was something to marvel at; and it was still feared by all who knew her.

She had never married, doubtless because no man ever had the temerity to try to tame her, so she lived alone in a tiny, gray cottage in a clearing of about an acre and a half on a high knoll at the confluence of two streams in the forest. She raised enough hay for her four sheep and enough potatoes for herself. She also kept ten hens, and a huge rooster that strutted about and crowed loudly and eloquently from dawn to dusk and always seemed conscious of the fact that he was the only male animal on the premises. She carded and spun the wool from the sheep and knitted it into socks and mitts, which she sold, and every month or so she sold a dozen eggs. For the rest she lived on the charity of her neighbors.

The young men of the community repaired her fences and her house, plowed her land, planted her potatoes, cut her hay and stored it in her tiny, dilapidated barn, and cut firewood for her stove. The young women came to cook and bake bread for her, to clean the house and to do her washing. Daily, she herself visited one or more of the nearer farms, and returned home with milk, cream, butter, bread, meat and sometimes discarded clothes. She was never in want so far as I know, and I never heard of her ever thanking any one for anything.

Old Betsy expected and accepted attention much as does the queen bee in the hive. She considered it her due. Nor did any one look for gratitude from her. All were content if she did not denounce them, but they could not be sure of that, for her tongue spared no one, not even those who had done the most for her.

In her own home Big Betsy was generous with what little she had, although no one ever visited her without bringing her a gift of some sort, or coming to do her some service. In the winter, if she did not appear about, a neighbor would tramp through the snow to see if she were still alive. Her home was so small, however, that she could not entertain more than three guests at the one time and these had to sit on the edge of her bed, for she only had one chair and that she occupied herself. Usually she served strong tea and bread and butter.

Her cottage had been built to her specifications many years before by the young men of the community and the frolic that followed was one of the gayest in the history of Washabuckt, with Betsy herself the gayest of the gay. I regret that I never made measurements of her cottage, but it was not more than eleven feet long by nine feet wide and the ceiling was so low that a moderately tall man had to remain stooped on entering until he sat on the bed. Of course there was only one room, and it had three small windows and a door. Besides the bed and the chair, it was furnished with a table, a wood stove that served both for cooking and for heating, and a wooden grocery box which held all her clothes and other possessions. The door faced south and on sunny days she kept it open and threw her slops out through it, so that the visitor had to approach it with caution. During the worst of the winter she kept her hens and her rooster in the cottage with her, not only to keep them warm but also to give herself company; and when the door was open the four sheep would stand in the entrance and gaze placidly and kindly at Betsy or her visitors.

Betsy's cottage was interesting to me for another reason and would be still more interesting today. It could have served as a museum of the early comic strips. She could not read or write, but she did love to look at the pictures in books, newspapers, and magazines. In the first days of the comics Washabuckters in the United States sent them to their folks at home when they were through with them, and they in turn gave them to Betsy when they were done with them. After she had looked them over she used them to paper her walls. Ultimately all four walls and the ceiling were covered with a choice collection of "The Yellow Kid," "Happy Hooligan" and other pioneer comic strips.

We boys were frequent visitors. We would haul water from the brook, cut firewood and pile it beside the stove, repair a fence and do other chores according to the season and Betsy's needs. That done we would spend an hour or more enjoying the comic strips, sometimes lying on our back on the bed the better to see them. We never tired of them. Our visits always ended with a swig from the bottle in which Old Betsy kept her "limin." This latter was no treat for us, but the old lady thought it was and insisted on our having it, so we had no choice in the matter. It was always easier to do what Betsy wanted done than to resist her.

Some years before, perhaps five, possibly ten, a kind visitor gave Betsy a lemon. It was the first and only lemon she ever saw, and indeed its remains were the only lemon that I ever saw in Washabuckt. This visitor explained how to make lemonade and dwelt on its merits as a drink, although he did not convince Betsy that whiskey was not better for her. Betsy did not understand the capacity and endurance of a lemon, and certainly this one was the most overworked lemon of all history. Betsy cut it in quarters and put it into a bottle with some water and sugar, and for years afterwards, until her death, she kept replenishing the water and sugar, and serving lemonade.

When I knew the poor old lemon it had taken on the complexion of an Egyptian mummy. It had lost all the vivid coloring of its prime and most of its vigor, but extraordinary to relate it still could be tasted and recognized. Betsy reserved the "limin" for her young guests. She took pride in telling them what a "limin" was and the vast distance hers had traveled in coming from "Celiferny." It was truly a remarkable "limin." But one swig of the bottle was more than enough.

OLD BETSY HAD a leading role in all Washabuckt social functions. No one could get married, hold a frolic, or get buried without her presence. She went everywhere, good weather or bad. It was never necessary to invite her, for she came anyway and made herself welcome. Once present she dominated the scene. She would sing and cheer on the dancers and the musicians, drink and squabble with the revelers, and wail and pray with the mourners. Her repartee was brilliant at times, and always sharp and cogent. Her appetite was good, even in old age, and she always took her fill of food and drink. She had vivacity and color; and on the slightest provocation she was explosive.

Even in her late eighties she tramped afoot nine

miles each way over rough and hilly country roads and spent a full day at a picnic at Iona to help raise funds for a new church after the old church had been burned to the ground. Not one of the hundreds present enjoyed the fun more than she did. She saw everything that was to be seen and did everything that was to be done.

Present was a blaring and thumping brass band from Sydney; and as it paraded about the picnic grounds the old girl led the paraders in its wake, waving her arms, swinging her cane, making remarks, some of them lewd, and cutting up generally. Asked afterwards what the band was playing she replied appropriately enough in her scant English:

"Damn, damn, damn, de picnic."

Father, eager to spend money to help the worthy cause, bought her tickets for some of the things being raffled; and she was the winner of one, a shiny, new bicycle. This caused some merriment, and some one suggested that she give it back to be sold for the church. This she refused to do. Instead she accepted it and pushed it all the way back to her home. She made several attempts to learn to ride it; and only stopped when Grandfather informed her that she was going to break her neck and that that would probably be a good thing for the community.

Above everything else at the picnic, Betsy was deeply impressed by the first phonograph she had ever seen or heard. As a matter of fact it was the first seen in that part of Cape Breton and impressed others as well as her. It was a varnished wooden box with a large metal crank protruding from one side, with some machinery on top, from which emerged a huge, bell-shaped horn. It sat on a table, and was exhibited by a bewhiskered old man, who did not know what made it operate, and kept shouting: "Come and see the talking machine! Come and see the talking machine! Come and marvel!" He would then put a cylindrical record on it, crank it, and set it going.

Soon a wheezing, blurred stream of sounds came from the horn that could with close attention be recognized as words or music, or a combination of both. As each record was played crowds would close in about the machine to listen and marvel, whereupon the old man would start to pass around a collection plate, and the crowd would disperse again. After this had happened for some hours, the crowd coming in backing away, like the surf on the shore, he complained to the parish priest. That benevolent gentleman spoke to the people, telling them what a great thing they were witnessing, and appealing to them to put some coins on the exhibitor's plate. Some did so while the pastor was there; but when he left their generosity left also.

When Big Betsy was told about the machine she would not believe it. Then when she saw it with her own eyes and heard the sounds with her own ears, she concluded that it must be possessed by the devil. What is more she said so, fortunately in Gaelic that the old man could not understand. When she was told that it was a church picnic and later when she heard the paster endorse the contraption she admitted that she might be wrong. She was not the only skeptic present. In fact some of the older people approached the machine guardedly. They simply did not trust it. They could not understand it and they could not explain it. Some felt that there must be a man behind the machine, or under it, that did the talking. They were certain that it was a trick of some kind.

While Betsy remained unconvinced, she could give a vivid description of it and its performance; and for years afterwards she entertained Washabuckt parties with her accounts of the talking machine.

OLD BETSY WAS the nearest thing that Washabuckt had to a historian in my time. She had a remarkable memory and could recount in detail the events of three or four score years before. She had been born in Scotland and had come to Washabuckt in infancy. She was the last of the pioneers living. The last of those that had come in maturity had died some years before, a lady who had passed the hundred-year mark and had lived beside a stream and was known as Jane Brook. Betsy had known Washabuckt from the days of the primeval forest, knew the faults and virtues of every person who had ever lived in the community, and loved to tell about the fights and frolics, tragedies and hardships of the early days. She delighted in recalling events long since forgotten. With no other living witness and no records to dispute her, her accounts of the old days kept getting more dramatic and more lurid.

The young men and women, especially, liked to hear her talk, for her knowledge of local men and events was intimate and she spared no one. They would ask her embarrassing questions and deliberately contradict her to stir her wrath, which was never difficult, so that they could hear her endless flow of Gaelic invective. She always obliged them by putting on a show. In its own way it had artistic merit, for she had been perfecting it for decades. Matching gesture to word, she would roar at times and at others she would hiss out terrible and biting words through her few, black teeth. Her language could not possibly be translated into English, for it had idioms and nuances of her own, and even if translatable it could not be printed.

Big Betsy to the end maintained a keen interest in romance. She never abandoned hope of landing a man for herself, and liked to be teased about her feminine beauty, and her wiles, and her way with men. She kept a sharp eye on the budding romances of the neighborhood and rarely missed one. She liked to embarrass shy boys and girls in love. When leaving a mixed gathering she would stop at the door, turn about and give one of the men a lewd wink with a nod of her head in the direction of the outdoors, and say: "Come to bush."

Her best show, however, was unconscious and usually unobserved. It was on the occasion when one of the hen-hawks in the nearby woods decided to make a raid on her hens. With much shrieking the hens would scatter and scramble for cover, and the proud rooster would stand his ground and defy the hawk to do his worst. In the middle of the storm Betsy would emerge from her cottage and damn and curse the hawk in words that would singe his feathers and in roars that could be heard for more than a mile in all directions. I never had the privilege of being present at one of these affairs, but those who had informed me that it could be compared only to some of the more violent convulsions of nature. A hawk never got one of Betsy's hens, but they kept on trying; perhaps they considered the old girl a challenge; or perhaps they, too, enjoyed the commotion.

Betsy's most precious possession did not exist. She got the idea, possibly some one suggested it to her, that there was a rich gold mine in the deep, wooded gulch back of her house. She reported far and wide that it had more gold than the Klondike. She was forever planning to extract some of the precious metal from it and make every one happy and prosperous. She would outline in graphic detail all the good she could do. There seemed to be no bounds to her imagination. The trouble was that she knew the fairies were stealing her gold. Here it was, according to her, that they refilled their crook of gold. She would stand above the gulch on evenings and roar at them.

Sometimes we boys would play the role of the fairies. With hammers or other metal tools we would sneak into the gulch. We would tap the rocks and generally make noises that would make Betsy think the fairies were again mining her gold. Soon Betsy would appear above us. She would curse the fairies to hell and denounce them as cheap thieves and blackguards. We would stop for some minutes and then resume the tapping and perhaps keep up the show for an hour or so. The next day Betsy would be about the neighborhood telling every one about the new visit from the fairies. Sometimes she would ask for volunteers to come and extract the gold before the fairies had stolen all of it.

The last time I saw Big Betsy she was ninety-six years old and confined to her bed. Neighboring women came daily to care for her and her hens and sheep. She was not ill; she was simply disintegrating. As it was, it was a wonder that any human body could have survived so long the strains and passion that hers had endured. She died a few weeks later.

CHAPTER THIRTEEN

The Private Life of the Sea Wolf

THE SEA WOLF WAS my boyhood hero before Jack London made him famous. In real life he was Captain Alexander MacLean, a distant relative of ours and a friend of my Father. He, and his brother Captain Donald, who figured in London's book as Death Larsen, were born and raised at East Bay on the Bras d'Or Lakes, and were well known in Cape Breton as great fighters and splendid seamen. Alec, or Sandy, as he was better known, was the more colorful and dramatic of the two and as a result the more famous and more popular.

The Sea Wolf was never discussed openly in Grandfather's family and in fact the relationship was admitted reluctantly. It seems, however, that Father, who had known both brothers from youth, maintained contact of some sort with Captain Alec for years, even when he was being hunted by three or four nations for his poaching, piracy and other depredations in the Pacific. Father's elder brother, Captain Alexander MacNeil, also made contact with him from time to time. When they visited Grandfather they would report to him on the Sea Wolf's activities. These reports usually were made at night, after the women folk had retired. I happened to eavesdrop on several of them. Later Father confirmed and amplified some of the things I had heard.

During the winter of 1899 the Sea Wolf lived with Father, who at that time owned and operated the Palace hotel at Bennett City, at the head of the route that led down the Yukon River to the goldfields of the Klondike and Alaska. There in the long Arctic night he told Father much of his experiences and of his troubles and of his ideas of things. According to Father everybody in Bennett knew who he was before the winter was out, and although there was a price on his head no one ever betrayed him. Perhaps no one dared to do so, for the Sea Wolf feared neither God nor man, and defied both.

An incident that happened in Bennett illustrates his courage. Among those staying at the Palace Hotel that winter was a notorious gambler, whose name Father mentioned, but which I cannot recall. This gambler cheated everybody with whom he played, and most of them knew it, but they played with him and accepted their losses in silence because he was a dead shot. Earlier in the winter one man had protested and was shot dead in the resulting duel. The gambler always played with two Colts on the table, one ready for each hand.

Some victims of the gambler arranged matters so that the gambler and the Sea Wolf got into a poker game. The word went around Bennett quickly and soon the saloon of the Palace Hotel was crowded. Some stood about the table watching the play and others stood nonchalantly at the bar, but with an eye in the direction of the table. They expected trouble. It was not long coming.

Captain Alec caught the gambler cheating, slammed his cards on the table, and denounced him for what he was in language that could not be misunderstood. The gambler rose quietly and slowly from the table, simulating what dignity and offended innocence he could, and challenged the Sea Wolf to fight it out with pistols.

Father pleaded with Captain Alec not to accept the challenge, for he felt it meant certain death, or at least to insist that the duel be fought with bare fists. The Sea Wolf was not much with pistols but he was a terrible man with his hands. Instead MacLean insisted on accepting the challenge on the spot and at once, named Father for his second. Aside he told Father not to worry about him.

Meanwhile the gambler picked the ace of spades from the deck of cards, walked slowly to the end of the saloon. The spectators lined up along the bar and the wall as he did so. At the end of the long room he stuck the card on a nail that protruded from the wall. He then turned his back on it and strode dramatically down the room, a pistol in each hand. When within a pace of the other end he turned quickly on his heel and fired one shot, almost without seeming to aim. The bullet pierced the spot on the card. As the card fluttered to the floor he shot again. The second bullet hit the falling card.

This was part of his show, a preliminary to every duel he fought, and intended to unnerve his opponent.

The gambler's exhibition of marksmanship did not disturb the Sea Wolf. He alone applauded it and offered congratulations. Then walking up to the gambler and his second he said:

"I don't know much about duels. Neither does my second. But I understand it is my privilege to name the distance."

"That's right," replied the gambler.

"All right then," bellowed the Sea Wolf, "You stand on one side of that table and I will stand on the other side. And you yellow-bellied son of a sea cook, you are not going to shoot first."

The gambler protested that that would not be a duel but a slaughter. A duel, he argued, should be a trial of skill, of marksmanship. But Captain Alec insisted on his rights, and the men in the saloon, all of whom were for him, supported him. The gambler then tried to get delay, to postpone the duel for a day or two. This again the Sea Wolf refused. He demanded that it be fought at once, right there and then. The spectators were enjoying the fun.

The strutting braggart turned coward. Captain Alec made him admit that he was a crook, a jail-bird, a wife-deserter and a murderer. He walked up to him and calmly took his two Colts and handed them to Father. That done, he battered and slammed the gambler about the saloon and finished up by throwing him out the door into the Arctic snow and cold.

That was the last Bennett City saw of the gambler.

While in the Far North the Sea Wolf tried in various ways to make a respectable livelihood, but fared none too well in any of them.

One spring he teamed up with two Montana miners, named Hustler and Brown, and left Bennett to seek a fortune in the goldfields. Nothing was heard of him for two months and then he returned to the Palace Hotel alone. The absence of Hustler and Brown was noted, but no one asked questions. Finally Father got the Sea Wolf alone and asked the big question.

"Oh, they just got sick and died," Captain Alec replied. That was that.

Nor did he fare any better in his regular profession. On his first arrival in the Klondike he commanded the *May Stratton*, a Yukon River steamer. He lost her in an ice jam between White Horse Rapids and Dawson City, but he saved all souls on board.

In the fall of 1902 he got a steamer of his own. A Captain Peterson of Bennett owned two steamers, the *Clara King* and the *Clara Monarch*. The Sea Wolf offered him $12,000 for the *Clara Monarch*. She was worth more, but as business was poor and the season late Peterson accepted. Captain Alec paid $6,000 in cash and gave a note for the balance. He hired some carpenters and fixed up accommodations for passengers on the *Clara Monarch*.

Late in October the Sea Wolf loaded his steamer to capacity with passengers and freight and headed down the Yukon for White Horse. Everybody predicted disaster in the ice; but he delivered them safely. Moreover, he reloaded her at White Horse and returned to Bennett with passengers and freight and with several scows in tow. It was an astounding exhibition of seamanship and daring.

River navigation, however, did not appeal to the Sea Wolf, and anyway he was yearning for his old haunts. He sought out Captain Peterson, paid him the remaining $6,000, and made him a present of the *Clara Monarch*.

Captain Alec then left Bennett for Tacoma, Washington, where he bought the *Carmencita*, later to be notorious over much of the Pacific. He took out Mexican registry for her and cleared her for Acapulco; but instead he headed for Neah Bay, Washington, where he met some of his old seamen and seal hunters. He never again deserted the Pacific.

While in the north the Sea Wolf also visited Nome, according to the report of Captain Alec MacNeil, who was there at the time and had known him from boyhood. Things were so wild in that wild spot, Captain MacNeil said, that the saner people were deeply concerned over conditions. Gambling houses, saloons, dancing halls, brothels operated without restraint. Crime and vice were open and profitable. Drunken men battled in the streets with fists or guns. Assault, robbery, and murder were daily occurrences. No one felt safe; and in fact no one was. Law enforcement had broken down so badly that no one could be found to serve as sheriff. Then the Sea Wolf came on the scene.

Some one got the happy idea of making him sheriff. It intrigued him, for he himself was sought by American,

Canadian, and Russian authorities, and probably also by the Australian, British, and Japanese. He was sworn in.

One after the other the new sheriff visited the scenes of Nome's trouble and gave his orders. That was enough. A deep and beautiful calm descended on the city. Daily the Sea Wolf patrolled the city, greeting everybody cheerfully and occasionally dropping into a saloon for a drink or something to eat. Everywhere he went he was saluted and admired. Nome at last had met its match.

The reign of the Sea Wolf did not last long, however, for he moved on and Nome went back to its old ways. With few exceptions, the people of Cape Breton who knew the Sea Wolf thought he was greatly maligned. Most of them spoke highly of him. His great strength and daring were admired and extolled, and most of those who had had dealings with him ashore found him gentle and kind.

THE RECORDS OF ST. MARY'S CHURCH at East Bay show that Captain Alec was born on May 15, 1858, and baptized on September 16, the same year; and that his brother Captain Dan was born on September 28, 1848, and baptized on November 12, the same year. The Rev. Michael MacCormick, the present parish priest and a noted athlete in his day, reports that their father Allan MacLean, and their mother, the former Catherine Mac-Cormick, were "good God-fearing people." The father died in 1870 or 1871 and the mother remained a widow until her death in 1894. He adds that the MacLean brothers attended the local school, but left East Bay in early manhood. The farm on which they lived has long been abandoned, but everybody in the neighborhood still speaks of the "great hospitality of the MacLeans."

Captain Alec was the benevolent gentleman on his visits to Cape Breton. Twice he crossed the continent quietly to see his own people while he was being hunted in the Pacific. He did not visit Washabuckt on those trips, although word of him reached the community. The way he scattered money about became a byword in Cape Breton. But what impressed me most deeply were the accounts of his enormous strength and of his colossal mustache. One seemed to go with the other, like Samson's strength and his hair.

According to the best information in Washabuckt the Sea Wolf's mustache had an antler-like spread of eighteen inches. Reports from the Pacific Coast say that he could tie both ends in a knot at the back of his neck. In two pictures of him on my desk as I write his mustache reaches his shoulder on each side, and in one the ends of it disappear down his back. Certainly his mustache was a sight to see, and something terrible when it bristled, as it was supposed to have done, when he became enraged.

The best testimony to the character of the MacLean brothers that I have found in a search of the records of sixty years, including the files of newspapers on the Pacific Coast, New York and Nova Scotia, and talks and correspondence with people who knew them in the flesh, was given by Ronald Gillis of Sydney, who wrote in 1942 from his sick bed in a hospital. Mr. Gillis had known Captain Alec from 1888 and Captain Dan from 1887, and while he had not sailed with either of them had been among their closest friends. His brother Hector had sailed with them on several voyages, including one notable trip when Captain Alec sailed his schooner from the Aleutians to San Francisco in eleven days, which would be a good time for a modern steamship.

Ronald Gillis wrote that Captain Alec stood about five feet, eleven inches, while Captain Dan was two inches shorter. The Sea Wolf, he said, was a splendid specimen of mankind, well-dressed as a "Spanish Grandee on parade," very active physically, and a good dancer. Both had rosy complexions. Captain Dan's hair was black, while Captain Alec's was fair. The Sea Wolf's eyes were either blue or gray, he added, but looked like "polished steel" when he was in action.

The best account of the Sea Wolf in action also comes from Mr. Gillis in a letter he wrote some time before for *The Sydney Post*, a letter that would have done credit to Jack London. In part it said:

"One fine afternoon he (Captain Alec) decided to go aboard his schooner.... The men, about eighty in number, were sprawled about the deck. He curtly ordered them below and padlocked the heavy door to their quarters. He ordered the cook to his galley and locked him in. Then he called his mate, a man by the name of McEachern, over six feet tall, weighing about 230 pounds, in fact a giant. He asked McEachern if it were true that he had let Captain Dan steal some of his best sealers. Being informed in the affirmative he quietly told him he was going to give him a licking.

"They both stripped to their underwear. Captain Alec laid his white starched collar and cuffs on the rail. He politely informed me that I could look on, but that there must be no interference.

"They fought up and down the deck; and I am sure that the men locked below would have been willing to forfeit a considerable part of their wages to have witnessed that fight. Since that day I have seen some of the world's champions fight but this surpassed them all, for it was a fight without gloves, without time out. At the end of thirty minutes McEachern said: 'I have enough.' He could not see. MacLean did not have a scratch on him. 'I have had enough too,' he replied quietly.

"He hooked his arm into McEachern's and led him down the cabin stairs. He ordered me to release the cook, and to have him bring hot water. He sponged and bathed the mate's injuries, as gentle as a child, and put court plaster over his cuts. Then the three of us had a drink together.

"Captain Alec then asked McEachern if he would get the men back. His reply was: 'If I don't, I won't sail.' The next day they headed up the North Pacific with the full crew aboard, and McEachern as mate."

This mixture of physical prowess and gentleness, of ardor in battle and kindness to the beaten enemy, appealed to the Cape Breton mind. This is what probably led Ronald Gillis to conclude:

"Captain Alec was not a Sea Wolf, as described by Jack London, nor was he harsh or cruel to his men, as long as they performed their duties."

How FAR THE SEA WOLF would go to help a friend who had helped him was shown in the libel action brought against *The New York Sun* in 1911 by Captain Nels P. Sorensen. The suit was based on an article written by William Churchill, associate editor, who some years before had been the United States Consul at Apia, in Samoa, and there had had experiences with both Captain Sorensen and Captain MacLean. Only one man, Captain Alec, could prove the facts in the article which concerned the joint activities of the two captains, and he could not enter the country because he was under indictment then for poaching on the sealing grounds of the Pribilof Islands. Mr. Churchill reached the Sea Wolf at Nanaimo, B.C. When Captain Alec heard his friend was in difficulty he dropped everything and traveled across Canada to Montreal, where he gave his testimony before a commissioner. This testimony won the case for *The Sun*.

As the records of the court tell an extraordinary story, and illumine one phase of the Sea Wolf's career, I shall give a brief summary of the case.

Captain Sorensen was a professional promoter of expeditions to the South Seas that promised quick and easy wealth to those who would invest in them. He and the Sea Wolf met in San Francisco in 1897. At that time

Captain Sorensen was promoting the South Sea Island Mining and Trading Company and Captain Alec had just taken over the schooner *Sophia Sutherland*, in which he had an interest, and was looking for adventure and gold. Captain Sorensen produced ore samples that he said assayed $5,000 a ton, and added he knew where there were large deposits in the Solomon Islands. They joined forces, Sorensen supplying the financing and MacLean the ship. They sailed for the South Seas in September. Aboard were fifteen or sixteen investors, mostly clerks and other workers who had put their little life's savings in the venture.

Apia was their first port. There Captain Alec visited the American consul. Mr. Churchill asked him what he knew about Sorensen, and the Sea Wolf had to reply that he knew little or nothing. Thereupon the consul told him that Sorensen had been in trouble in Australia for a similar expedition, and produced a Captain Hamburg to prove it.

Thus put on guard, Captain Alec inquired about his partner from various officials at British ports in the South Seas and learned nothing good and much that was bad about him. MacLean, however, went ahead with the expedition's plans. He got the proper licenses and did some digging at the sites proposed by Sorensen. They did find some traces of gold and copper, but none in paying quantities, and nothing assaying anything like $5,000 a ton. The Sea Wolf decided to get rid of Captain Sorensen and return to San Francisco.

First he proposed to leave his partner behind, but he found the British authorities were as eager to be rid of him as he was. Then, he said, he made an agreement with a British Commissioner. He declared that he gave that official two pounds in gold to pay Sorensen's fare to Australia. As a ship was due in two weeks, he added, he put him in a hut on a small island in the Solomon group with enough food to last that time. Mr. Churchill, however, testified that Chief Justice Chambers of Samoa told him that Captain Alec and the crew of the *Sophia Sutherland* tied Sorensen to a tree on the island and whipped him unmercifully with a rope. Moreover, added Mr. Churchill, this was the story that the Sea Wolf himself told along the waterfront of Apia on his return there. Captain Sorensen denied all this. He insisted that everything was beautiful. He testified that he and Captain Alec parted the best of friends, after Captain Alec had given him two sovereigns to pay his fare to Australia.

Anyway Captain Sorensen and Captain MacLean parted. Ten days later malaria hit the crew of the *Sophia Sutherland*. Many of the men died. For two weeks the Sea Wolf sailed the ship single-handed, something for the record books. When he brought her into Apia again he had only four living men aboard and they were all sick. There he saw Mr. Churchill again, and reported the expedition a complete failure.

Somehow Sorensen got safely away from his island. Ten years later he turned up in New York with the idea for a new expedition. This one was to dive for $20,000,000 in sunken treasure in the South Seas. Mr. Churchill recognized him as his old acquaintance of Apia, and wrote the article exposing him that resulted in the libel action.

An account of another of the Sea Wolf's expeditions to the South Seas, and a more characteristic one, was given in an article in the *Vancouver Province*, shortly after his death in 1914, by Tom McInnis, a reporter who had known Captain Alec for many years. It seems that McInnis and a lady named Vanilla had dinner one night in 1896 with the Sea Wolf in the Poodle Dog, a restaurant in Victoria, B.C. McInnis in part wrote:

"That night his manner was gentle and his words carefully chosen. He was evidently much impressed by

Vanilla. It was only after the wine that his tongue was loosened to tell us some of his experiences.

"MacLean took out of his pocket a small chamois bag, like a miner's poke for gold dust but shorter. He rolled out eleven pearls on the tablecloth and they glimmered in the rice which he had packed in the bag with them. Most of the pearls were round and creamy and very sizable for rings. Two were like clouds of indigo touched with the moon. One was a large, pear-shaped, salmon-pink pearl. Vanilla was greatly taken with that one. Naturally she asked how he came by them. He answered that he got them honestly and openly as a poacher in the South Seas.

"His story was that a friend who was indefinitely confined at San Quentin had secretly passed out information to him in gratitude for a favor, and having faith in what was told to him, he outfitted a schooner and sailed across the Pacific for a little island owned by the French. At this island there was a season for pearling every ten years. It was now the ninth year and the oysters were in a profitable condition. The trick was to get there and away without being noticed by any prowling French gunboats.

"One morning they sighted an island as indicated by the chart he had received. MacLean had men with him who knew just what to do and were equipped for quick work. So they went at it in the hot sun and brought the oysters up against time.

"About four o'clock of the afternoon of the third day a trail of smoke was seen on the horizon. It was approaching the island. With all possible speed the opened oysters and bottom debris on deck were put overboard, together with the pearling dredges and prongs, and every trace of what they had been so busy at was removed. They had been lucky; there were many fine pearls. These they imbedded and covered in the pitch of the ship's seams. By the time the French gunboat sent officers aboard to investigate they found only an innocent little trading schooner preparing to send men ashore for a supply of cocoanuts and to catch some fresh fish along the reefs.

"The French officers, however, were very stubborn. Orders were issued for the schooner to cast off and follow the gunboat to a French police and penal station on a distant island. There was no help for it; a shot or two from the guns in those remote waters and the incident would be closed. The Sea Wolf had to navigate under orders from two men left on board. The gunboat itself was old and slow.

"The second evening after the capture the gunboat stopped for the night at an island and entered a lagoon. The schooner followed.

"The darkness settled, breathless, ominous and without a star. Evidently a storm was brewing, but all was safe within the lagoon. There was a cable between the gunboat and the schooner. Only two men were left aboard the gunboat, the rest of the men and officers having gone ashore to visit a small native settlement. The storm came down suddenly and heavily.

"Under the direction of the Sea Wolf the two men on the schooner were overcome without any outcry. The cable was slipped. The crew manned two boats and drew ahead pulling the schooner. Presently by the help of the oars and the wind the schooner reached the mouth of the lagoon and glided out into the stormy ocean.

"It was blowing great guns outside but that was all to the taste of MacLean. Sails were hoisted and they were away before the crew of the gunboat had realized what had happened. Out through the raging black seas they went, the Sea Wolf did not care where so long as he was in the open. No gunboat followed and they ultimately reached the coast of Australia.

"The next time I saw Vanilla she showed me the pink pearl. I asked her if she were going to have it set in a ring or a pendant. She replied that she would not tell me, but that I might find out before the Captain sailed away. And so it was that when I said good-by to the Sea Wolf he was self-consciously but proudly wearing the pink pearl in his tie, neatly set in five golden claws."

These ventures for gold and pearls were only interludes in the career of the Sea Wolf. His favorite occupation, and mainstay, was poaching for seals on the bleak, cold islands of the North Pacific. There he defied the cutters of the Czar of Russia and of the United States. He sailed many ships, all of which he owned in whole or in part, and he flew the flags of many nations, including practically all of those of the Central American republics. For a time he flew a flag of his own design. With equal unconcern and daring he defied the storms and ice floes of the Bering Sea and ignored the laws of all nations. He made his own laws, in fact, and would invoke these to deal with some daring seaman or hunter who had the temerity to pit himself against his skipper. He was bold and picturesque at all times and sometimes cold and brutal. At sea he drank and cursed and read philosophy.

When he wanted to be rid of a man he would put him ashore on some remote island, or if an island were not near, simply throw him into the Pacific and tell him to swim to shore.

"It was not my fault," he once told Father of a man he threw overboard, "if he could not make it."

While in the Yukon, Father asked him how many men he had killed up to that time. He denied that he had ever killed a man, and this is still believed by some of his relatives and friends surviving in Cape Breton. He explained, however, that he had lost fifty-nine of his men, which was probably an understatement.

Captain Alec's career in the Pacific started in 1880, after he and his brother had sailed ships around Cape

Horn from Nova Scotia. It is known that he and Captain Dan coasted the shores of Alaska in 1883 in a seven-ton sloop. On their return to San Francisco the two brothers took the schooner *City of San Diego* on what was probably the first sealing cruise into the Bering Sea. They discovered many rookeries and returned with 900 sealskins. Next Captain Alec was master of the *Mary Ellen*. Shortly afterwards he bought the *J. Hamilton Lewis*, and with this ship started his career as an outlaw. From then on he was a marked and hunted man.

Ultimately news of Captain Alec's raids on the seals reached civilization and the Russian government sent the cutter *Alexander* to capture him. After a long and cold and dangerous search the *Alexander* finally located him. At the time he was within the three-mile limit and thus subject to Russian law. The commander of the *Alexander* signaled the Sea Wolf to show his papers:

"Come and get them, if you are big enough," responded the poacher.

The Sea Wolf had a fast ship and a daring crew, so he spread sails and headed for the open seas. The cutter took up the chase. After ten miles the cutter came within shouting and firing range of the *J. Hamilton Lewis*. Captain MacLean hove to, for the cutter could sink him. Instead of surrendering he lined up his crew on the deck, each man armed with a rifle, and hoisted the American flag. That done he shouted to the Russian commander:

"Now fire and be damned to you."

With that he dipped his colors three times. He was now on the high seas and he knew his rights. The Russian knew them, too. He dipped his colors in reply and left the scene. There was nothing else he could do without risking an international "incident."

Later the same season the Sea Wolf encountered the Russian cutter *Aleut* on the high seas. Again he was asked to show his papers; and again he refused. Once more he fled and the cutter gave chase. This Russian commander fired shots at Captain Alec's ship, and finally boarded her. After a hard tussle and many injuries, but no deaths, the Sea Wolf and his crew were subdued. They and the ship were taken captives to Petropaulovski. There Captain Alec spent four months in prison.

On his release he brought suit against the Russian government, much to its embarrassment. When it was clear that he was going to win, the Russians paid him heavy damages to be rid of him, his ship and the suit.

On still another occasion the Sea Wolf had an interesting affair with the Russians. He was in Vladivostok. At that time that port was a mess of mud and dirt. Plank sidewalks lined the streets, and on them people moved about the town. The place was garrisoned by one of the swank regiments of the Czar. When the bemedaled, bespurred, and gaudily uniformed officers strutted down the plank sidewalks, ordinary people had to step into the mud to allow them to go by. Everybody did so until Captain Alec arrived.

One afternoon the Sea Wolf was "doing" the town. As he was strolling along the sidewalk he encountered three officers, walking abreast, in step, and mighty proud of themselves. As the Sea Wolf did not budge, they walked right into him. That started the fight, and the three officers landed on their heads in the ocean of mud, medals, spurs, gaudy uniforms and all. The regiment was called out; and it was needed to subdue Captain MacLean.

The Sea Wolf did not favor Russians, for at various times he was in trouble with the British, the Japanese, the French, the Canadians and the Americans. He did not discriminate among them. And he commanded many ships on many expeditions. Besides those already mentioned these included the *Rose Sparks*, the *Webster,* the *Alexander*, the *Bonanza*, the *Acapulco*, and the *Favorite*. He also liked to vary his activities, and these ranged from taking cargoes of illicit liquor to the natives in the Far North to transporting high explosives. He would do anything except freight a cargo of ordinary, legal merchandise.

His death was as strange as his life. In the early days of World War I he moored the *Favorite* in False Creek, an inlet of Vancouver Harbor. To board his ship, one had to cross over the decks of two other ships moored beside it. Returning one night Captain Alec is believed to have fallen between two of the ships, and in doing so to have hit the gunwale of one of them. Anyway, his dead body was found the next morning lying in three feet of dirty water between two of the ships. It was thought at first that he had met foul play, but the Coroner's inquest on September 5, 1914, disproved this. It was also brought out that he had been cold sober. In the great turbulence in Europe his death passed almost unnoticed.

J ACK LONDON'S BOOK gave the Sea Wolf a reputation that he did not relish, and he certainly would not have liked the two Hollywood motion pictures based on it. While reticent on the subject it is known that he got and read the book, and he did comment on it at various times.

How London went about presenting a copy of the book to Captain MacLean was told by Noel Robinson in *Sea Lore* in 1935. He wrote that he got the story from the Sea Wolf himself. One morning just before the Sea Wolf was to leave San Francisco for the sealing ground, he relates, he met Jack London in a chandler's office on the waterfront. The novelist had come to wish him luck on his venture. Just as they were saying good-by London handed the Captain a parcel with the remark: "Open this, Alec, when you are on the sealing grounds and smoke my health." They shook hands and parted.

Some months later Captain Alec was visited by another sealing skipper in the Far North. The Sea Wolf went to his cupboard to get a glass of grog for his guest. There he noticed the box given to him by Jack London. He unwrapped it and sure enough it was a cigar box. Turning to the visitor he said: "Let's smoke Jack's health." He opened the box only to discover a book entitled *The Sea Wolf*. Later he read the book, and recognized himself in the role of Wolf Larsen.

At the time, Mr. Robinson added, he saw "red," but in later years rather liked the book.

Father got a different impression. The Sea Wolf did not like any part of the book, Father said, and had two major objections to it. First he objected to being made a "Swede" and secondly he objected to being killed off in the final chapters after a sound licking.

Tom McInnis confirmed this view. He declared that in 1907 the Sea Wolf had complained bitterly to him of how Jack London had maligned him. He added that Captain Alec had expressed the hope that he might be able to shanghai the novelist, and if he did he would put him through "his paces" in a way he had never treated any other man.

Captain Alec was questioned on London's book in his testimony in Montreal in the Sorensen case. The sealing part of the book resembled some of his experiences, he said, but added that he was not the "brutal, violent man" that Wolf Larsen was pictured to be.

"In writing the book," he testified, "I suppose Jack London had to take somebody in it, and I suppose he took me. I have never objected because I have never met London since."

183

CHAPTER FOURTEEN

St. Ann's Big Boy

GRANDFATHER'S HERO WAS the Giant MacAskill. As a young man he had seen him several times and had been so deeply impressed that he had never forgotten the slightest detail about him. Nor would Grandfather let anybody else forget about him either, for he loved to tell about his immense size, his feats of strength, and the colorful and astounding things he did or said. When any one spoke of other champions or of heroic deeds, Grandfather always brought up the Giant MacAskill and overwhelmed him.

Colossal as were the Giant's physical dimensions, these were not so extraordinary as was his enormous strength. He was not one of those freaks of nature caused by some glandular disorder. He was not one of those tall, stringy, clumsy, stupid, sickly reeds of a man that are so often exhibited in the touring circuses of America. He was well-proportioned in body, with breadth and depth to go with his height, and a mind that was above average. He was big in everything, and well-balanced.

This was why he was esteemed so highly in Cape Breton by all classes of people, for if the average Cape Bretoner admires anything it is physical prowess. Evidence of this may be found on every hand. When the Cape Bretoner speaks of heroes he speaks of strong men. When he refers to his ancestors he does not brag about their kindliness, their intelligence, their bravery, although he might well do so, but about their physical strength. The stories about the early settlers that survive almost invariably tell of battles with bullies or with a hard climate.

Take for instance the *History of Christmas Island Parish*, by Archibald J. MacKenzie. Mr. MacKenzie is dealing with the church to which the early settlers of that part of the Bras d'Or Lakes, including those of Washabuckt, had to travel over miles of wildness, or over the waters of the lake, for spiritual consolation, and so he is primarily concerned with their faith, but over and over again he dwells on their bodily strength. Some of the anecdotes that he relates are interesting as well as illuminating.

Of Angus MacNeil, better known in Gaelic as Aonghas Ruairidh or Angus Rory, one of the strong men of Piper's Cove, he writes:

"Perhaps there were others who were fully as strong as Angus, but none so full of life as he. Standing on the floor of his father's home, he could spring up and strike the ceiling with the heels of his boots and come down on the floor again on his feet. One day while at St. Peter's when some parties raised Angus's temper to the fighting point, he made a sudden spring and planted his two heels above the door of one of the stores. Shortly afterwards a man named Donald McDonald (Big) who was working on the canal got on a rampage and challenged to fight the best that ever went there from Grand Narrows and Iona (settlements near Piper's Cove). Angus heard about this and accepted the challenge at once. It was agreed to that the fight should be staged in a field west of the town at 7 P.M. that day. Hundreds gathered to see the fight, expecting no doubt to see a long, hard battle. But such it did not prove to be. There was only one blow struck. In the beginning of the first round Angus made a drive at his opponent, struck him in the region of the heart, lifted him off his feet, and landed him in a helpless condition about a dozen feet from the place he was standing. The fight was over."

Of Allan MacNeil, a blacksmith, known in Gaelic as Ailean MacEachainn, or Allan son of Hector, he writes:

"Like all his brothers he was noted for his great strength, and he could make good use of it when the circumstances demanded stern action. Shortly after he went to Arichat to learn his trade he and a friend were taking a walk one afternoon when they met a number of men including a noted French bully who was in the habit of acting in certain ways in the presence of Scotsmen to insinuate that they needed a remedy for the itch. MacNeil did not know at first what the bully meant, but when his friend told him about it, his blood began to boil. He coaxed his friend, who was an able man, to trounce the bully, but he would not venture. When the bully heard them talking he went over to them and said to MacNeil: 'Can you play the Scotch fiddle?' For reply he got a blow in the side of the head that knocked him senseless and made the blood pour from his ears. His comrades left him on the ground where he fell and fled, and Mac-Neil had to go to work to revive the bully. It is safe to say that this incident taught him a lesson as to the danger of insulting a Scotchman, and it is said that he governed himself accordingly ever afterwards."

CAPE BRETON HAS LONG BEEN NOTED for its big men and its strong men, but the Giant MacAskill was its superlative specimen. In a race of big men he stood, as it was so aptly put, "a lighthouse amid lampposts"; and in a race of strong men he was a Samson. He was seven feet, nine inches tall, eighty inches around the chest, and his shoulders spanned forty-four inches. The best information seems to be that in his prime he weighed 425 pounds, although there are reports that he weighed more than 500 pounds. His hand was twelve inches long and six inches wide, and one story about him has it that once when he was asked to take up a handful of tea, he picked up a pound. One of his shoes that still survives is eighteen inches long. His eyes were blue and his hair fair. He was completely beardless.

A worthy biography of him entitled *The Cape Breton Giant*, was written by James D. Gillis, a noted character in his own right, and it has become one of the most precious items of Cape Bretoniana. Mr. Gillis was well qualified for his work. He had taught school in Cape Breton for many years, and had lived among its rural Scottish people most of his life, although he does write in his brief sketch of himself: "I was twice in the United States; I do not say so for the sake of boast." Mr. Gillis visited St. Ann's and tracked down most of the legends about the Giant. His book is complete and authoritative, one might say definitive. As he himself writes in the introduction: "The author is satisfied that this work is virtually a superb representative of MacAskill's greatness."

Much of what follows is based on Mr. Gillis's authority, for no one could write about the Giant without referring to him and his book. The rest of it is based on memories of my Grandfather's stories of his hero. At times they differ in detail but never in major matters.

Angus MacAskill was born in 1825 in Harris, the southwestern part of the Island of Lewis, in the Hebrides, not far from Barra. His father and mother and his nine brothers and three sisters were of normal size. When the Giant was six years old the family migrated to America and settled in St. Ann's, for, as Mr. Gillis says, "In those days America was the Boston, the Whycocomagh, or the Klondike of today." In Cape Breton Angus grew apace, both in size and strength, although there was nothing unusual about his life or diet excepting that he ate a large bowl of oatmeal porridge after each meal. Of this Scottish dessert Mr. Gillis remarks: "It slams the door on the dwarf's nose in the days of growth."

On reaching maturity MacAskill used both tobacco and liquor in moderation. One of his smoking pipes still exists, and it is worthy of its owner. It is made from the trunk of a cherry tree, with one of the limbs forming the stem, and holds a sixth of a pound of tobacco at a filling. For his grog he used a wooden dish known as a "tub" that would hold three normal drinks.

As the Giant grew he helped his father and his brothers with the work of the farm, plowing, harrowing, planting, reaping and caring for the stock. He got along well with his neighbors and with the other boys. He went to school, attended the local Presbyterian Church, and read the Bible on Sundays. He led a quiet, peaceful life, troubling no one. In fact there was no one in the neighborhood who would taunt him. One bully came some distance to challenge him to fight, hoping thereby to win some reputation, but the Giant refused to do battle. Instead he asked him to shake hands. He grasped the bully's hand so firmly that he crushed it, and made it useless.

From early youth he gave evidence of his superhuman strength. When only sixteen years old he alone lifted a huge log that was to be sawn into boards by hand and placed it on a frame seven feet above the ground, a task that would have tested the strength of seven men. On another occasion one of a team of horses took ill and collapsed while plowing. He unhitched the horse, took its place, and went on plowing for hours.

Perhaps the best story of the Big Boy's strength is one told by Mr. Gillis, because it is also a clue to the Giant's character.

It seems that one of the humble men of the neighborhood implored a local merchant to let him have a barrel
of flour on credit so that his family would not starve. Finally the merchant, to get rid of him, told him that there
were some barrels in the hold of a vessel at the wharf
and that he could have one or all of them if he or any
other man could throw them out of the hold. Evidently
the merchant did not know of MacAskill or of his will-
ingness to help a friend in trouble. The humble man went
to the vessel, and found the hold was twelve feet deep.
On his way home, disconsolate, he met the Giant and
told him of his trouble and of the merchant's offer. Angus and the man went direct to the vessel. The Giant
went into the hold and hurled barrel after barrel out of
the hold, and clear of the deck of the ship into the waters
of the harbor. There were six barrels in all and the needy
man drove home with all of them to his family.

MacAskill's fame spread far and wide. Finally it
reached the ears of Phineas Taylor Barnum in New
York. The famous showman sent an agent to St. Ann's
and the Giant joined his circus. With it he toured much
of the United States, Canada, Cuba, England and Scotland. The colorful Barnum, whose sense of the extraordinary has never been surpassed, teamed MacAskill with
the equally famous Colonel Tom Thumb, who was supposed to be the smallest man living, and probably was.
At times Tom, the midget, would square off in the circus
ring, and challenge Angus, the Giant, to battle, much to
the amusement of MacAskill and the spectators. At other
times Angus would carry Colonel Thumb about the circus on the palm of his extended hand, on which Tom
would do a step dance. At still other times Angus would
pick up his tiny companion and put him in his pocket.

While the show was in London Angus MacAskill
was commanded to visit Queen Victoria. That august
lady, small and pudgy herself, wanted to see the biggest

and strongest man in her far-flung empire. She received him cordially in Buckingham Palace and plied him with questions for an hour or more on his size, his strength, his home, his life and his aspirations. She made a favorable impression on the Giant, but what impression he made on her has not been preserved for posterity. As he was departing she gave him a ring of gold. Mr. Gillis says she gave him two rings.

Cape Breton legend gives its own characteristic touch to the reports of the royal interview. According to this, the Giant was eager to display his strength to the queen, but for a time could not think of any way of doing so politely. Finally he got an idea. He rose from his seat and walked up and down the chamber in front of Her Majesty with great dignity and deliberation. As he did so he pressed his heels firmly into the deep, soft, carpet, and those big heels cut footprints into it like tracks in the Nova Scotia snow.

In the British Isles MacAskill also went to see the huge claymore with which Sir William Wallace slaughtered the English on many battlefields. He saw it all right and was allowed to handle it. The report goes that he brandished it about in great sweeps, and afterwards remarked that while he could swing it he would not want to do so all day as Wallace had done, although nine inches have been broken off it, so that it is both shorter and lighter than when it was wielded by the national hero of the Scots. The original was seven feet long and weighed forty pounds.

According to Grandfather's version all this happened in the Tower of London, where Wallace was executed. I had heard him tell the story time and again, so that it was fixed in my memory, and I shall never forget how the old man would rise to his feet and slash the air in great swipes as he demonstrated how first Wallace and then MacAskill handled the great sword with easy dexterity.

This later caused me some embarrassment.

In London in 1935 for the Silver Jubilee of King George V, I visited the Tower of London to see the Wallace sword. I looked over the great and interesting collection of arms in the Tower, but could find no trace of it. I had felt certain that it would be prominently displayed, for certainly all visiting Scots would wish to see it. Ultimately I asked one of the Beefeaters, the guards of the Tower, where it was. He had never heard of it. He called another Beefeater, one who had spent his life with this collection, and he, too, knew nothing of it. I asked for the curator, presented my credentials, and insisted on seeing it. Neither did the curator know of it. He suggested the Governor of the Tower. The latter and his minions could find no record of it in the Tower. I was then referred to the Department of Antiquities in one of the Ministries. There was still no record of it. Officials took my address and promised to track it down.

Some months after my return home they did locate it. It had never been in the Tower. The official letter explained with a humor that is unusual in such correspondence that his English captors did not dare to have Wallace and his sword in London at the same time, so it was taken from him and left in a castle at Dumbarton, where it remained for some centuries before being returned to Edinburgh. I wrote a letter of apology to official England for the trouble I had given to it, explaining that I had been so insistent because I had suspected a dire English plot to hide the great Scottish treasure. Later I looked up Mr. Gillis's book and found that he had the facts correctly stated. It was the first time that I had found Grandfather wrong in anything, and this was twenty-five years after his death.

Like so many other Cape Bretoners the Giant MacAskill had a deep love of the sea and when he could not be on it liked to be near it. But Barnum did not want him wandering about, for he felt that people were not going to pay good American cash to see his Giant when they could see him for nothing. So MacAskill did not get about as much as he would like; but when he did he usually made for the waterfront.

On one occasion—reports say it was in New York—the Giant was strolling towards the docks when he met a friend of his from Cape Breton, who had had an argument with some of the natives about MacAskill's strength. Together they walked into a saloon, where some of these arguers were still loitering. Angus ordered a round of drinks. While the others were having their drink he strode over to a 140-gallon puncheon of rum that was standing on the floor. He hit the top of it a rap with his knuckles. The bung popped out and hit the ceiling. Then he picked up the puncheon and had his own drink out of it. He paid for the round of drinks, his own included, and with his friend walked quietly out of the bar.

As they left one of the native New Yorkers was heard to say:

"We should run him for Congress."

Another visit to the New York waterfront was the Giant's undoing. There are many versions of what happened and while they differ in details they agree in essentials. It seems that one evening Angus was on one of the docks talking to some seamen. Nearby was a heavy anchor. One version by Mr. Gillis says it weighed 2200 pounds and another by him 2700, while Grandfather simply said that it weighed a ton. Anyway it was a heavy anchor. For some reason, there being no agreement on it, MacAskill lifted the anchor to his shoulder and walked up and down the dock with it. When he let it slip off his shoulder, however, one of the flukes caught him in the shoulder, or the side.

Angus was never the same again. He suffered intense

pain at the time, and the reports say that some of the spectators actually wept at the sight. He may have broken some ribs. He may have suffered internal injuries. He may even have fractured his spine. His trouble was not properly diagnosed for there were no X-rays in those days. He never could stand completely erect again. He quit Barnum and returned to St. Ann's.

With the modest fortune made in his public life the Giant started two gristmills in the neighborhood of St. Ann's and opened a general store in the village. For a time he himself operated one of the mills, and it is reported that he would toss about three- and four-bushel bags of grain and meal as if they were pound packages of tea or sugar. It is also reported that at times when the waterpower for the mills gave out and the people needed their meal Angus would turn the great grinding stones himself. He preferred to run the store, however, and seated on a 180-gallon molasses puncheon he would discuss public affairs and entertain his customers and admirers. His ledger is still extant and shows that he had a sound knowledge of business. He made a reputation for fair dealing.

His business career was short-lived. He was stricken with "brain fever" and died on August 8, 1863, at the age of 38, amid general mourning. Two carpenters were set to work to build the coffin. It was so large, remarks Mr. Gillis, that it was found "sufficient to bear or float three men across the Bay of St. Ann's." His grave, a mound of earth twelve feet long and four wide, is still visited by many people yearly, who come to see and marvel.

How the Giant MacAskill impressed and still impressed native Cape Bretoners was expressed by Mr. Gillis in these words:

"In his own realm of greatness he was the Bonnie Prince Charlie, the Wallace, the Bruce, the Napoleon Bonaparte, the Marshall Ney, the Wellington, the O'Conel, the Robert Burns, or the Washington of his countless friends, according as they happened to be impressed by the different phases of his greatness."

Grandfather's appraisal was less fulsome: he merely classed the Cape Breton Giant with Samson and Hercules.

Publisher's Afterword

THIS NEW EDITION of Neil MacNeil's *The Highland Heart in Nova Scotia* celebrates fifty years of a remarkable Cape Breton Classic. Told with the brave, bold strokes of a combination of pride and solid information, *The Highland Heart* is pioneer history writ large, with all the purity and bravado and passion that only an exiled native son can bring to the world of his childhood and of his heart.

And this is wonderful writing—exuberant, rich, overstated and humble—telling us of the peace and invincibility, vulnerability and raw humour of a pocket of the Golden Age of Celtic Cape Breton's rural life. The contradictions are many, as they must be—the over-told story keeps alive what is essential; it has the stretch that suggests the truth—and those who know the Cape Breton kitchen racket know the bawdy jokes and good time teasing, the retold story honed toward the classic in being told again and again. *The Highland Heart in Nova Scotia* is the Washabuckt of Neil MacNeil's heart, the stories of indelible winter evenings, the background for dreams. It's the whitest whites and the blackest blacks—and of course, the strongest of the strong.

And Neil McNeil was there. When he writes about the now lost economy of daily Cape Breton life, we are getting firsthand information. There's no bluster or bluff in that. Through it all, small minds get their comeuppance and pomposity gets leveled in rip-

roaring stories that continue to roar fifty years after Neil MacNeil
dared to put them on paper.

BORN IN DORCHESTER, MASSACHUSETTS, February 6,
1891, Neil MacNeil came as a young child to live with his grandfather in Washabuckt in Cape Breton's Victoria County—the journey
that sets the scene and tone for *The Highland Heart in Nova Scotia.*
His father, John MacNeil, travelled Canada and the United States as
a building contractor. He was part of the Yukon Gold Rush in the
1890s and helped rebuild San Francisco after the earthquake. His
son Neil grew up in Washabuckt, eventually graduating from St.
Francis Xavier University in Antigonish.

Fluent in Gaelic, he was proud that he spoke it with a Barra accent. In Gaelic he was known as Michael John's son, after his grandfather Michael and his father John. English-speaking Nova Scotians
knew him as Neil F., for Francis, a middle name he never used. In
the one-room school in Washabuckt, there were three Neil Mac-
Neils in Primary, two of them Neil F. So our Neil was called Neil
Bras d'Or because he lived by the lake, and the other boy was Neil
Baddeck.

Both of Neil MacNeil's parents were MacNeils—John A. and
Catherine—and both families came from Washabuckt, Cape Breton,
across the water from Baddeck. John A.'s people arrived in Cape
Breton in 1818, and Catherine's probably came about the same
time—both families from the Island of Barra in the Outer Hebrides at
the time of the collapse of the kelp industry after Napoleon's defeat.

Neil F.'s mother's father's father was a Washabuckt carpenter.
Shortly before the American Civil War, this carpenter's four sons
went up to the Boston States. They were Hector, Michael, John and
Neil MacNeil. Neil is said to have served in the Union Army, and
after the war he and his three brothers formed the MacNeil Brothers
construction company. Their shop on Atlantic Avenue was wiped
out in Boston's great fire of 1872. The company re-opened in Dorchester and was based there until the firm closed in 1913.

Neil was the youngest of the four brothers, and he outlived the
others by many years. Hector died in 1869, Michael in 1886 and

John in 1896. All three left children. By the mid-1880s, the firm had become enormously prosperous, building many structures in Boston, Cambridge and elsewhere. They built many of the cottages in Newport, including the Vanderbilts' "The Breakers." The firm made great sums of money, and offered work to young men from Washabuckt and Iona. And as his brothers died off, Neil (who had no children) took charge of their children and their share of the firm, saw to it that the sons got an education. Several of these young men went to St. Francis Xavier University in Antigonish in the 1890s, and Neil became a major contributor to the college. For instance, the science building—MacNeil Building—is named after him (even though he was the only brother who spelled his name "McNeil"). Eventually, Neil (called "The Millionaire" in *The Highland Heart in Nova Scotia*) had about nineteen nephews and nieces—one of whom was Catherine, the only child of John MacNeil, and the mother of our author Neil MacNeil.

While it sounds good told here, the reality was that Uncle Neil was sole owner of MacNeil Brothers, and the nieces and nephews all became his dependents. But that's another story....

ONE OF THE YOUNG MEN who came from Washabuckt to work at MacNeil Brothers was John A. MacNeil. He married Catherine, the daughter of Neil's brother John. They had four children: our author Neil Francis (born February 6, 1891), a daughter who died as an infant, another daughter Lucy, and a son Murdoch, who died at the second battle of Ypres, 1916.

While still in Cape Breton, Neil MacNeil became a newspaperman. As he tells us in *The Highland Heart in Nova Scotia*: "I was appointed the Washabuckt correspondent of *The Victoria News*. Weekly I gathered local personal items and mailed them to the editor; for which I got no pay but the honor and the experience. I shall never forget the thrill of seeing my first efforts in type. I was also thrilled by the fame and dignity my writing brought me in the community. Perhaps journalism was in my blood; anyway it became my life's work."

After graduating from St. Francis Xavier University (1912), Neil MacNeil took a job selling insurance in Newfoundland, with a singular lack of success. By 1914 he was a reporter and soon city editor for the *Montreal Daily Mail*. He transferred to the *Montreal Gazette* as military editor in 1916. Next year he became New York correspondent for the *Gazette* and the *Toronto Globe*. Except for a year in the U. S. Army, he was on the staff of the *New York Times* from 1918 to 1951. He was at different times national editor, foreign editor, city editor and finally assistant managing editor. His first journalistic triumph was his realization in 1922 that an unopened grave in Egypt was a major discovery. It was King Tut's tomb. From 1932 through 1948, MacNeil headed the *New York Times* staff at all the national political conventions of the two major parties in the United States. In 1951 he received the John O'Hara Cosgrave medal for distinguished service to journalism. And he held honorary degrees from St. Francis Xavier University (1947) and from Catholic University (1955).

Neil MacNeil wrote other books, including: *Without Fear or Favor* (1940), *How to be a Newspaperman* (1942), and *An American Peace* (1944). After his retirement, he became editorial director (at a dollar a year) of the second Hoover Commission to reorganize the federal government, writing (with Harold W. Metz) *The Hoover Report, 1953-55*. He was former American President Herbert Hoover's literary executor.

But it is as the author of *The Highland Heart in Nova Scotia*, first published in 1948, that Neil MacNeil will be long remembered. For depth, detail, and outrageous good humour, this is probably the best home-grown book about Cape Breton Island. And fifty years since it was published, it tells 100-year-old stories that are fresh today.

Neil MacNeil died in Southampton, New York, on December 30, 1969.

Ronald Caplan
Wreck Cove
1998

CONTINUED ON NEXT PAGE

WATCHMAN AGAINST THE WORLD
by FLORA McPHERSON
The Remarkable Journey of Norman McLeod and his People from Scotland to Cape Breton Island to New Zealand
A detailed picture of the tyranny and tenderness with which an absolute leader won, held and developed a community— and a story of the desperation, vigour, and devotion of which the 19th-century Scottish exiles were capable.
$16.25

ECHOES FROM LABOR'S WARS
by DAWN FRASER
Industrial Cape Breton in the 1920s
Echoes of World War One
Autobiography & Other Writings
Introduction by David Frank
& Don MacGillivray
Dawn Fraser's narrative verse and stories are a powerful, compelling testament to courage, peace & community. They belong in every home, in every school.
$13.00

CAPE BRETON QUARRY
by STEWART DONOVAN
A book of poetry that gravitates between rural and urban Cape Breton Island, and the experience of working away. Stewart Donovan has written a relaxed, accessible set of poems of a man's growing up and his reflections on the near and distant past of his communities.
A lovely, lasting little book.
$11.00

SILENT OBSERVER
by CHRISTY MacKINNON
Born in Cape Breton over 100 years ago, deaf at the age of two, Christy MacKinnon recreated her childhood in her own words and paintings. A family book— hardcover, 39 full-colour illustrations.
$23.50

HIGHLAND SETTLER
by CHARLES W. DUNN
A Portrait of the Scottish Gael
in Cape Breton & Eastern Nova Scotia
"This is one of the best books yet written on the culture of the Gaels of Cape Breton and one of the few good studies of a folk-culture."—*Western Folklore*.
$16.25

CASTAWAY ON CAPE BRETON
Two Great Shipwreck Narratives
1. Ensign Prenties' *Narrative* of Shipwreck at Margaree Harbour, 1780 (Edited with an Historical Setting and Notes by G. G. Campbell)
2. Samuel Burrows' *Narrative* of Shipwreck on the Cheticamp Coast, 1823 (With Notes on Acadians Who Cared for the Survivors by Charles D. Roach)
$13.00

THE CAPE BRETON GIANT
by JAMES D. GILLIS
& "Memoir of Gillis" by Thomas Raddall
A book about not one, but two singular Cape Bretoners: Giant Angus MacAskill and Author James D. Gillis.
"Informative, entertaining, outrageous...!"
$10.00

MABEL BELL:
Alexander's Silent Partner
by LILIAS M. TOWARD
The classic biography—a new edition with large, readable type and glowing photographs. Told from Mabel's letters and family papers, this is their intimate story of love and courage. With bibliography.
$18.50

CAPE BRETON CAPTAIN
by Captain DAVID A. McLEOD
Reminiscences from
50 Years Afloat & Ashore
A rough-and-tumble autobiography of sailing, shipwreck, mutiny, and love.
$13.00

CONTINUED ON NEXT PAGE